ADAMS

CREATIVE NEGOTIATING

Other Adams Media Business Books

ADAMS

CREATIVE NEGOTIATING

Proven Techniques for Getting What You Want from Any Negotiation

STEPHEN KOZICKI

Adams Media Corporation
Holbrook, Massachusetts

Published by
Adams Media Corporation
260 Center Street, Holbrook, MA 02343

ISBN: 1-55850-797-3

Printed in the United States of America.

J I H G F E D C B A

Library of Congress Cataloging-in-Publication Data
Kozicki, Stephen.
    Creative negotiating : proven techniques for getting what you want from
any negotiation / Stephen Kozicki.
        p.   cm.
    Includes bibliographical references and index.
    ISBN 1-55850-797-3
    1. Negotiation. 2. Persuasion (Psychology). I. Title.
    BF637.N4K68   1998
    302.3—dc21   97-44937
                                                        CIP

Contents

Acknowledgments

They say that the movie *Ben Hur* was a mighty big production. This book has really become "bigger than *Ben Hur*," and I would like to thank a number of people for their help and professional contribution: Doug Malouf, Thais Turner, Margaret McAlister, W. T. McCabe, Allan Stomann, Nigel King, John Leftwich, Greg Hooper, Phil Shorten, Allyn Day, and, of course, Gillian for her patience and understanding!

Foreword

Most of us negotiate every day.

Teachers negotiate their value to school authorities and students.

Doctors negotiate healing their patients.

Parents negotiate their way of life with their children.

It's clear: the essential skills of the nineties are those that help us understand and deal with other people. We need to recognize and develop those skills—and the knowledge contained in this book will help us to do just that.

Few people know the art of negotiation as well as Stephen Kozicki. As I have watched his career develop, I have encountered person after person who says: "I wish I had Stephen's skill with people." One day, after agreeing with yet another satisfied customer that Stephen Kozicki is indeed a talented negotiator and communicator, I said: "Look, Stephen, I think it's time you shared your knowledge around a bit. There are lots of people out there who wouldn't mind knowing how you get such good results. Why don't you put it in a book?"

Stephen, it seemed, had been thinking along the same lines. So off he went and authored his first book. When I saw the results, I was happy both for Stephen and for his future readers. His friendly, approachable style will ensure that they learn the basics of successful negotiation the easy way—without having to wade through paragraph after paragraph laced with jargon and theory.

Stephen is one of the most successful and knowledgeable negotiators in the world. His advice works. But more importantly, he can show you how to achieve great results without having to resort to shady tactics, trickery, or manipulation.

That is what being a truly talented negotiator is all about.

The advice in this book is timely. Current research demonstrates that communication is becoming a lost art.

We don't really listen to people.

We don't concentrate too well.

We have stopped talking to our neighbors.

We don't talk to strangers.

This book will help us all to move out of the comfort zone. It will encourage us to listen more and to negotiate more, instead of just arguing—or giving up. After all, we're all pretty much the same under the skin: we all have the same basic needs and desires. To satisfy these needs, we need to understand and negotiate with others.

The great Dale Carnegie, in his book *How to Win Friends and Influence People*, urged us to open up; to be more outgoing. Stephen Kozicki has taken this excellent advice and expanded on it. Listen to others—then modify, adjust, and evaluate what we hear. In other words, negotiate.

Yes, you can get a better deal; a stronger relationship; a pool in the backyard; an angry neighbor off your back—if you are prepared to negotiate.

Creative Negotiating is a book that will become an indispensable part of your library, fitting right into the list of essential business and communication books of the nineties. I am so proud to be associated with its author, Stephen Kozicki.

— DOUG MALOUF

Introduction

Negotiation is really a simple procedure. It's basically a matter of two sides sitting down to reach an agreement—a solution that, ideally, will leave both sides happy; the classic win/win solution. I like to think about negotiation as being the art of reaching an agreement by resolving differences through creativity.

Put like that, it might make you wonder why I felt the need to write a book called *Creative Negotiating* in the first place. If it's so easy, why a whole new book? Aren't there plenty of books on negotiation already? Why do we need another one? I wrote it for these reasons: first, many of the books currently on the market make negotiating seem a lot harder than it is. It is a simple procedure. *Creative Negotiating* provides you with an easy, step-by-step process to follow that will lead you to negotiating success. The process revolves around:

A flexible negotiating style (moving along a continuum from quick to deliberate). Carefully planned outcomes (realistic, acceptable, or worst possible). Adherence to the following four basic principles:

1. There are no rules.
2. Everything is negotiable.
3. Ask for a better deal.
4. Learn to say no.

You will learn how to follow a Negotiation Model through four phases of the investigation and develop a plan that provides a sound basis for the final agreement.

The second reason I wrote the book is I wanted to show that negotiation can (and should) be a creative process. There are endless ways to reach a creative solution. For the truly skilled negotiator, there is no place for the dog-eat-dog attitude advocated by too many unimaginative negotiators. Once you realize that the needs and drives that spur you on are shared by the other side, you will be able to use this knowledge to work with, rather than against, the other party, to reach a mutually satisfying agreement.

Finally, I wanted to bring home to all of you out there—from the astute businessperson to the homemaker shopping for a new refrigerator—that absolutely anything and everything can be negotiated. It doesn't matter whether we are talking about furniture or international agreements. All businesses are prepared to negotiate a better price, a better delivery date, better terms—if you know how to go about it.

You now have those simple secrets in your hands. You'll be amazed at what you can achieve when you hone your negotiating skills. Lucrative contracts for your goods and services will be a reality instead of a dream—and you don't have to browbeat others, or use sneaky tactics, to achieve what you want.

Picture creative negotiating as walking a tightrope of your own design, a rope that flexes to accommodate as the process of negotiation rages around you. A rope that supports your "balancing act" in the contemporary negotiating process.

A sound knowledge of negotiating skills, allied with a genuine respect for the needs of the other party, will make a tremendous difference in your life. I know it has in mine—and in the lives of others with whom I have shared this knowledge in the past. So take my advice: don't just read this book, use it—and begin to appreciate the magic of creative negotiation.

— STEPHEN KOZICKI

Chapter 1

The Columbus Technique

Imagination is more important than knowledge.

—Albert Einstein

Next time someone asks you if you're a member of the Flat Earth Society—start worrying. What they're telling you, ever so subtly, is that you're stagnant.

You're not perceptive.

You lack vision.

In effect, they are telling you that if Columbus hadn't proved that the world was round, you'd still be worrying about sailing off the edge of it on your next vacation cruise.

Luckily for the world, Christopher Columbus had vision aplenty. Some 500 years ago, he was lying awake at night picturing himself sailing around the world, discovering new trade routes. He knew the world was round. But to set sail and prove it, he needed support and funding from the royal family. Unfortunately there were one or two problems in the way.

For one, the Flat Earth Movement was alive and well. Everyone happily agreed that the world was flat and that, moreover, everything worth discovering had already been found. For another,

Columbus hadn't a major discovery to his name. To most people he was an unknown.

This was not a great position from which to start negotiations. Christopher Columbus, however, adventurer and visionary, didn't let that deter him. He decided to come up with a plan so tempting that Queen Isabella and King Ferdinand couldn't say no.

Canny Christopher knew perfectly well that the royal family wanted to see their own interests served. There was no way they were going to back something that was likely to cost them a lot of money with no return—or worse still, make them look gullible. But new trade routes . . . increased wealth . . . now that was tempting.

Nor was Columbus prepared to beg and crawl for the chance to prove he was right without making sure that he was going to come out of the deal okay as well. He knew the way to succeed was to put himself and the royal family into a win/win situation—although it's unlikely that he put it in quite those terms!

Let's take an admiring glance at his technique. First of all, he was totally convinced that he was right—the world was round, not flat. But he was well aware that just "knowing" you're right doesn't mean others will take your word for it and happily do whatever you want. By the time the vital meeting came around Columbus had tried to consider all possible angles.

When he presented the plan to the decision makers, he bargained over his involvement in the adventure. Not only did he ask for ships, he also asked for appropriate honors, various titles, and even a percentage of the trade obtained from the new trade route! Don't you think his supreme confidence that there would be a new trade route probably had a great deal to do with the successful outcome of his negotiations? After all, Queen Isabella would be asking herself, why would he be pushing for a percentage of the profits if he were not pretty certain there were going to be profits?

In the end, even after having to walk away from the negotiation, Columbus closed the deal with an agreement that allowed him substantial gain. Queen Isabella was happy. Columbus was happy. It was a triumph for the win/win outcome in the negotiating process.

It's not likely your negotiations will have quite the impact of those of Columbus. Thanks to him, the New World was discovered and settled some time ago.

But you can use the Columbus Technique to negotiate your way to success. You can have a satisfying outcome each time. Regardless of whether your negotiations are about where the family should spend its next holiday, a pay raise, or an international supply agreement, the Columbus route leads to success.

Let's have a closer look.

The technique

First of all, Columbus understood only too well that a negotiation can take place only when everyone involved thinks that he or she will get some benefit from the transaction. In a nutshell, both sides want to be in on the deal. Once you realize that, it's just a matter of a few refinements.

This is where the negotiating process really begins. It's a place to be creative. Write this out and put it somewhere where you can see it:

> *Negotiation is the art of reaching an agreement*
> *by resolving differences through creativity.*

If we put the deal pulled off by Columbus under the microscope, we can see that he

paid careful attention to detail, and
clinched the deal by being creative.

The process revolved around these three things:

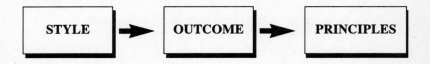

For convenience, we will refer to these (somewhat unpoetically) as S.O.P.'s. They are as relevant in today's negotiations as they were 500 years ago.

STYLE

Most people have no idea how important style is in a negotiation. They enter into each and every negotiation in the same way. This is not only time-consuming but counterproductive as well. After all, you don't treat all your friends and acquaintances exactly the same way, do you? Isn't there someone you know who's a bit more sensitive than most—so you have to be extra careful not to hurt their feelings. Or what about that member of the family with such a thick hide that you need to be appallingly blunt to get the message across?

Everyone's different. Every situation is different. So you vary your style of negotiating according to the person with whom you're dealing and according to what you want out of the deal.

There are two main styles you can choose from to start any negotiation. Both will make the process more productive and successful.

It's helpful to have a model against which to measure the desired outcome. Think about style as being on a continuum, allowing you flexibility in your choice of a style to use at any given time. At one end is the Quick style; at the other end is the Deliberate style; and right in the middle is the Compromise style. In this book we focus on the extreme ends of the style continuum.

Without realizing that the two styles exist, it's difficult to know

(a) where to start a negotiation, and
(b) if you've achieved the best outcome.

You also need to know when to turn on your heel and simply walk out of the discussions. Sometimes the outcome is simply not going to be worth the effort involved to close the deal.

The Quick style

Use this style when you need to negotiate in a hurry. The main consideration: you will not (or not within the foreseeable future) be doing business again with that individual or organization.

A characteristic of the Quick style is that it's fairly competitive. Both the buyer and the seller take a position; neither wishes to move from that position.

For instance, say your old refrigerator has seen better days and you have to replace it right away. You go to a large department store—and you see IT immediately: the Deluxe Frigidaire. Your dream fridge. Ice on tap. Auto defrost. Love at first sight. The ticket says it's yours for $1,850.

You tap your teeth reflectively. You think for a while. You check your account balance. Then you head down the road to Harry's Specialty Electrical Store.

There's the same fridge. The ticket says $1,875, but Harry is ready to make a deal. How do you go about it?

If it makes you uncomfortable, you don't have to haggle as though you're in an Eastern bazaar. All you need to say is:

"If I decide right now, what's the best price?"

You'll be surprised at how much Harry will knock off the price to get your business! And at the end of the transaction, you can ask him to throw in free delivery!

Remember—you use this style for a quick decision. No long-term business relationship is involved. By the time you come back in five to seven years to buy the Frigidaire's more sophisticated cousin, Harry will probably have sold out to someone else.

We've seen the Quick style's usefulness in buying something like a house, car, furniture, and so on. But it is essential to realize that those who succeed in business or in relationships negotiate on a continual basis. Sometimes the Quick style is not appropriate. (In fact, sometimes it is a disaster!)

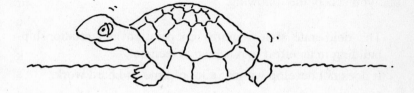

You must know, then, when to use the Deliberate style of negotiating.

The Deliberate style

You've probably guessed that if the Quick style is for use when there's no ongoing business commitment, then the Deliberate style comes into its own when you want to develop or maintain a long-term relationship: when you realize the importance of a deal that satisfies both parties.

The key to the Deliberate style is knowing that the business will be ongoing—for months, years, or even decades. What does this mean in regard to your negotiating style? Basically, it means that you accept the following:

The deliberate style requires cooperation and relationship-building in an effort to reach an agreement.

It does not develop without a lot of time and hard work.

It means moving forward, sideways, backward, and back again!

An experience of mine some years ago illustrates the Deliberate style in action. I was negotiating an agreement with a large bank in Australia for the supply of computer hardware and consumables for all of Australia and part of the Pacific. After many meetings the bank's purchasing manager issued a contract for the agreement. As we were about to sign the agreement he paused.

"Just one thing, Stephen," he said. "Our Service Department uses a lot of consumables. They're not too happy about the discount price." He waited.

Pushing aside the instinctive feeling of frustration that welled up, I carefully studied the whole situation again. I could see that by altering just one delivery we could make up the difference.

With a bit of creativity we solved the problem: he got his higher discount for the department; I secured a lucrative contract. A contract that exceeded my expectations for supplies by 40 percent in the first year alone!

Were we both happy? You bet.

As you can see, the right choice of style will greatly affect the outcome of any negotiation in which you become involved.

Here is a summary of the two styles:

Quick Style	**Deliberate Style**
Time constraints	No time concerns
One-time meeting	Many meetings
Short-term relationship	Long-term relationship
Price main consideration	Many issues and variables
High emotions	Controlled emotions

Remember the continuum:

The best position for starting any negotiation is right in the center. Once you decide to move to either end of the continuum, it's not a big jump, but a gentle move either way. To use this approach successfully, you will need to remain flexible at all times.

I have seen many deliberate negotiations turn into a quick negotiation and then back again in a number of hours. This process continues until agreement is finally reached. Just because you decide to adopt a Deliberate style does not mean the other side will see it the same way.

The decision about which style to use is in direct proportion to the desired outcome of the negotiation. If you go charging into a negotiation with the approach "I-know-what-I-want-and-I'm-

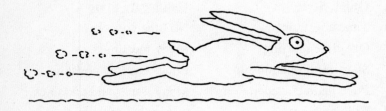

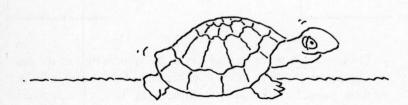

going-to-get-it-at-all-costs," then you can expect an outcome that reflects such lack of planning and consideration.

If Columbus had tried this approach with Queen Isabella and King Ferdinand, the outcome of the meeting would probably have been vastly different. Had he gone in with only the thought, "I want royal approval to set off to look for a new trade route," the negotiation would likely have been far more one-sided. In that frame of mind, he would have agreed to anything remotely enticing.

Outcomes vary with each style—and preparation is the key. The question of the desired outcome is as serious as your choice of style. So let's move to the "O" of the S.O.P.s'.

OUTCOME

As with the different styles of negotiations, there are various outcomes that can occur:

REALISTIC OUTCOME
ACCEPTABLE OUTCOME
WORST POSSIBLE OUTCOME

It's necessary in any negotiation that you decide what you want from a deal and go for it.

Don't stubbornly set your sights on one result only.

Why?
Because research findings are showing this:
Negotiators who have a number of predetermined outcomes have a better chance of getting what they want than negotiators who aim only at the best result.
Aim high, yes—but spend time preparing more than one desired outcome.

Realistic outcome

This is the best result—both parties are satisfied by the transaction. You may see this result from either the Quick or the Deliberate style of negotiating. Here we have the classic win/win outcome: both sides feel they'd like to do business again. This is the outcome for which you should strive in every situation.

Although it can and does happen that both sides have that win/win feeling after a quick negotiation, you would usually find that this kind of outcome is the result of the Deliberate style, where both sides are working together in a creative manner to achieve a Realistic outcome.

Remember the bank purchasing manager who asked me for a better price? In this case, the bank's negotiator used the classic negotiating tactic of adding a "nibble" to the end of the discussions. It was only by adopting a creative problem-solving approach that the contract was saved. By looking at the delivery and changing the minimum order requirement, I was able to secure the contract.

The result? A personal and professional achievement on both sides. We both felt that the agreement was satisfactory, and a Realistic outcome to our negotiations.

Acceptable outcome

As we move down the scale the outcomes start to represent more the Quick style of negotiating. In the case of the Acceptable outcome, you will get to the end of the negotiation and feel that, while the deal might be acceptable, you could have got a better outcome. Don't waste time on such thoughts; they're entirely counterproductive.

Here's a little experiment for you to try:

The next time you go to buy a product, go to four similar establishments and check the prices. You'll probably be startled to note major differences. In most cases someone has sat down and, with a series of pen strokes, created a price. Again in most cases, people accept these pen strokes as a legitimate price that cannot be challenged!

It can. Ask for a better price. You will be pleasantly surprised.

To test my claims, I encouraged my wife, Gillian, to ask for a more favorable deal from a number of stores. Without question, each store gave her a better price! The improvement ranged from five to twenty dollars. By the end of the week she was up to nearly sixty dollars. (Pity I wiped out the family profit with a parking ticket the same week.)

Always ask for a better deal. Businesses are always keen to move a product or a service—it's better than nothing.

It's an Acceptable outcome.

Worst Possible outcome

You can be faced with the Worst Possible outcome in both negotiating styles, but it is far more common when you're using the Quick style. For instance, if you're trying to negotiate a better price in a retail store and receive a resounding NO, it's probably because you're trying to negotiate with someone who doesn't have the authority to vary the terms.

The result? A lose/lose situation. You lose because you don't get the product or service; they lose because they didn't get your business. This is the Worst Possible outcome for both parties.

If you have been using the Deliberate style of negotiation and get the Worst Possible outcome, it's usually because someone becomes emotionally involved in the process. Is there any need to spell out how dangerous this can be? I have seen companies lose thousands of dollars due to managerial ego standing in the way of a good deal. I bet you've seen it yourself: reason tends to fly out the window when someone's ego is on the line.

Creative problem-solving doesn't have a chance—because someone is standing there stubbornly with only one thought paramount:

"I'm absolutely right and you're definitely wrong."

Much as you prefer not to think about it, this could happen to you. You can indulge in a bit of mental sleight-of-hand here to

improve your chances; however, if the Worst Possible outcome is considered as an option, then it is far easier to make a decision and look for creative solutions.

Many, many negotiators invite the Worst Possible outcome because of their method of planning—or more accurately their lack of planning. Would you believe that an astounding percentage of negotiators do their planning on the way to the negotiation? Then, when their gamble fails and the Worst Possible outcome seems about to eventuate, they press the panic button and the deal ends in disaster.

Think carefully, think creatively, and think ahead.

Write this on a card and keep it where you'll see it often.

For instance, it might be more creative for you or the company to think of a "poor" result not as the Worst Possible outcome, but as the first outcome. If you make a deliberate decision, a small deal today may be the beginning of a long relationship. In this case, the establishment of the relationship is what counts.

What does it all mean?

When you looked at style, you found that you could move along the continuum between Quick and Deliberate, according to the development of the negotiation.

You can work the outcomes the same way. You will find yourself moving up or down the scale depending on the timing of the negotiations and the style you are using.

The true negotiating professional is always looking at ways to be a problem solver in the process of trying to find the best deal. Rather than slamming a fist on the table and making outrageous demands, he or she looks at creative alternatives.

To bring it all together, look at the chart below. By combining elements of style and outcomes, you have the freedom to move around. Like Columbus, you can plot the best trade route!

Use the Columbus Technique in your next negotiation. You will be able to plot the style, plan for the desired outcomes, and start to get a feel for the likely result.

In all your negotiations, the best position to adopt is the one right in the center of both continuums. This will enable you to become the classic "Creative Negotiator" with a problem-solving approach to the process.

THE COLUMBUS TECHNIQUE

PRINCIPLED NEGOTIATION

In an ideal world, everyone would have high principles and unimpeachable business ethics. Regrettably, we don't live in an ideal world. I have seen wonderful people lose considerable amounts of money because they mistakenly believed that the other side would look after their interests.

Try this: fix the following four principles firmly in your mind before you walk into a negotiation. You'll have a much greater chance of guaranteeing not only survival, but success.

There are no rules

I often hear the "Negotiating Process" being referred to as the "great game of life." Game? This is a misconception that a lot of people have about negotiating. Whenever I have been involved in a deal in which the other party treats negotiating as a game, they have lost.

Why?

Because they have assumed that rules are present.

They have assumed they would not get stung.

These assumptions don't hold water.

Don't ever take it for granted that just because you make a generous concession, the other party will do the same thing.

There is, however, a way to overcome the "no rules" trap. Establish an agenda very early in the negotiation process. This allows you to work within certain parameters and keep reasonable control.

Everything is negotiable

Absolutely anything and everything that you can think of is available to be negotiated. Relationships, products, services— even life can be negotiated.

Most people accept printed documents every day, without question, from lawyers, accountants, doctors, government departments, and large companies. However, all of those businesses would be prepared for you to negotiate a better price, better terms, better delivery date. Remember, this refers to substantive issues in the negotiation, not the other side's principles, or yours.

If you adopt the philosophy that everything can be negotiated, then you will be surprised how often you can obtain a mutually satisfying agreement. Just because something is printed on an official document or a price is written in gold ink in an exclusive shop, don't think those terms are etched in stone.

Ask for a better deal

There are direct parallels between why people don't negotiate and why salespeople are reluctant to ask for the order. It is because of a conditioned fear—the fear of hearing the word "NO."

We don't like anyone saying no to us, so usually we try not to put ourselves in the position where someone can reject us. If you're someone who has never tried to negotiate, try the procedure I suggested to you earlier in the chapter. Practice by going to a few stores and getting a price on a new refrigerator. You will find that the price will vary from fifty to two hundred dollars.

Then go one step further. Go to the lowest-priced retailer and try asking for an even better price. It's more than likely that the price will come down again! Go on. Try it—and welcome to the world of negotiating! You really can ask your way to success.

Learn to say No yourself

Conversely, in a negotiation you should be prepared to say no and put a halt to the proceedings. The mark of a disciplined negotiator is the ability to say no and walk away. I have seen a number of negotiations where the deal was a bad one (actually going far beyond the concept of the Worst Possible outcome), but because the parties had invested so much time and ego, neither was prepared to say no—so a disastrous deal was struck.

Many years ago, I heard about an executive who traveled to Japan to close a deal. The right result, he knew, would secure for him a promotion in his company.

He had a week to conduct his negotiations. The Japanese were good hosts, and on his arrival in Tokyo politely took his airline ticket to confirm his return flight.

Have you guessed the outcome? That's right—because they knew the time of his return flight, the real negotiation did not take place until they were on the way back to the airport.

He was shocked by the offer, but signed the deal anyway because of the pressure of time invested in the process. He should have said no, no, and NO!

On the surface of it, it appeared that the result was the Worst Possible outcome for him and the best possible for the other side. Actually, both lost as neither party did business again.

I met that executive recently when I attended an international negotiating course in New York.

"All I needed to do was say no," he said ruefully. "But the thought of going back to America without the deal was just too much. Anything seemed better than nothing."

Learn to say no and you will not only survive, you will ultimately have far more success in negotiating. It's an interesting phenomenon, and true. I am sure it's repeated every day in every nation around the world. There are times when a "no" deal is better than a terrible deal. Really, the ability to say no means that you have planned, and the "no" deal is a prepared outcome.

How did Columbus use his style, outcome, and principles?
(S.O.P.'s)?

The first thing Columbus realized was that it would be a partnership deal with the royal family. He could see that negotiations would be a long, deliberate process. Then, having decided on his negotiating style, he went about being creative in his presentation, and aimed at a Realistic outcome. Knowing the principles involved, he just hung in there for the deal he wanted.

It was nearly seven years from the start of the negotiations until he was on board the *Santa María* ready to sail. Columbus sets us an excellent example of how to establish a long-term business relationship that will succeed.

However, Columbus's S.O.P.'s changed dramatically when he was looking for men to crew his ships. You can imagine the laughter in the taverns when he suggested he was sailing to the end of the earth and beyond! No room for lengthy, deliberate negotiations there. All he needed was a crew—unlike the negotiation with Queen Isabella, where he needed to create a long-term relationship.

With the crew, time was not important. It was straight in, negotiate, and then on to the next tavern. Christopher Columbus assuredly did a lot for international trade, but he also gave us a very good model to use when negotiating!

It's a pity Columbus wasn't around in 1989 when the Pilot's Federation in Australia commenced an infamous strike. His advice would have been useful in the negotiations. The pilots went into the dispute with very high demands and expected a quick resolution. The problem? They wanted a Realistic outcome with a Quick style.

The two don't mix well.

Then the issue became more complicated, when the then Prime Minister came on the scene. He, too, wanted a Realistic outcome—but he also wanted to use the Quick style. With two angry, diametrically opposed sides, you can imagine how well this was likely to work. History shows it didn't.

You can probably think of other examples where someone could have saved the day by being prepared to negotiate a better solution. Observe and learn from other people's mistakes. Are you prepared to go into your next negotiation with a problem-solving approach, prepared to find creative solutions—or are you still of the belief that table banging and having a louder voice than the other side will win the day?

SUMMARY

The global market today is not kind to the unseasoned negotiator. For your own protection—and the good of your company—you need to become battle-hardened. If you have a low pain threshold when it comes to negotiating, then all you can do is practice, practice, practice.

What if you are asked to negotiate for your company, and you know that you are not motivated toward negotiating? Do your company a favor. Tell someone. If you are not motivated toward the dynamics of negotiating, you can better serve the organization by staying away from the negotiating table.

Every negotiation you become involved in will be different, but the basics of what we have discussed so far remain the same. There are no tricks to be learned. It really is just a matter of practice for negotiating to become second nature.

Negotiating is an everyday occurrence, and it is a skill that you can learn very quickly by applying the Columbus Technique. Developing this skill allows you to have a better quality of life, because it will take away the tension that normally exists when someone says:

"Let's negotiate!"

THE COLUMBUS TECHNIQUE

Remember the S.O.P.'s . . .

STYLE
- Quick–Deliberate

OUTCOME
- Realistic
- Acceptable
- Worst Possible

PRINCIPLES
- There are no rules
- Everything is negotiable
- Ask for a better deal
- Learn to say no

Chapter 2

Are You a Motivated Negotiator?

Quality is a habit, not an act.

—Aristotle

Naturally you want the best possible deal for your side every time you sit down to negotiate. This being so, it doesn't take a great stretch of the imagination to realize that the people sitting on the other side of the table feel exactly the same. They are just as motivated as you are, and possibly more so.

Spend a moment thinking about the messages you received about winning as you were growing up. Think about sports, study, games, finances, career. Think about your friends' attitudes to these activities, too. It's probable that most of you are conditioned to think that winning, in any competition, is the most important part of the game.

Negotiating is no different.

Unfortunately, the problem with the "win-at-all-costs" mindset is that it fails to recognize the needs of the other negotiator. If both sides enter into a negotiation with that attitude, it's no surprise when tension fills the air.

In chapter 1, we looked at how Principled negotiation (the Deliberate style) provides an alternative to Positional (or Quick style) bargaining. Principled negotiation, explored initially at the Harvard Negotiation Project some years ago, is explicitly designed to produce wise outcomes efficiently and amicably.

The process of Principled negotiation can conveniently be divided into four parts:

1. People
2. Interests
3. Options
4. Criteria

The People component is one that we'll be taking a closer look at. We'll see how the needs and drives that spur us on in the negotiation process are shared by both parties. It is essential that we be able to step back and separate the people in the negotiation from the negotiation process itself.

When you understand what really motivates you, it becomes easier to understand what motivates others. This understanding is the key to being able to work with, rather than against, the other party to solve the problem and reach a mutually satisfying agreement. These principles hold whether we are talking of individuals or nations.

A simple illustration:

You can understand that if the other side's basic need is for survival, it would be a waste of time to push achievement as the motivation.

Let's imagine that one day you find yourself in the situation of having to negotiate with a terrorist. Would you assume even for one second that his immediate needs were the same as yours? Obviously, you would need to negotiate at different levels—it would be most unlikely that he would be worrying about his growth as an individual.

Fortunately, in most commercial negotiations, our basic needs for survival and security are well catered to. We look for different needs to be fulfilled: needs for growth, accomplishment, or achievement. Your own personal needs will have great influence on how you approach the negotiating process, and on the results.

THE AREAS OF NEGOTIATION

Just what does determine success or failure when you first look someone in the eye across the negotiating table?

There are six broad areas you need to look at:

1. Enthusiasm
2. Recognition
3. Integrity
4. Social skills
5. Self-control/teamwork
6. Creativity

Enthusiasm

Enthusiasm is contagious. Rest assured that any half-heartedness or fear on your part will be picked up by the opposition; it's impossible to be on guard all the time against body language. Unconscious movements or expressions on your part will tell others if you're tired, dispirited, angry, or indifferent. People pick up all sorts of subconscious cues.

✓ Program yourself. Think about what the deal means to you, your career, your self-image, and the company. Regard a difficult negotiation as a challenge, and approach it in a spirit of competition—competing not only against others, but against your own record. In your mind, run through all possible outcomes so you will be prepared, but concentrate on the best outcome. Aim high. Let that confidence and enthusiasm shine through.

Recognition

What does the successful completion of the deal mean to you? It should mean some form of recognition, such as approval from others ("Good for you, Terry, you pulled it off!") and/or financial reward commensurate with effort. You should walk away with a glow of pride over your accomplishment.

If you don't receive recognition from others—or even acknowledge your own achievement—you're in the wrong job or the wrong company.

✔ If recognition is a problem, sit down and do some serious thinking. What do you want out of your job? What do you want from the company? Where do you see yourself in five years' time? How much money do you need/want over the next five years? Make time to set some clear goals.

Integrity

Never compromise your standards to clinch a deal. Yes, we did say earlier you should assume "there are no rules"—but that's for self-defense.

If you stoop to trickery or deception you'll hang yourself eventually.

It doesn't take too long for the word to get around. Apart from the risk of being known as someone who is unethical—or worse, a con artist, your own self-image will suffer.

Develop a reputation for you and your company of integrity, trustworthiness, and helpfulness. Not just skin-deep pleasantries either, but genuine concern for the well-being of the other party.

✔ Go the extra mile in every situation—find extra information, follow up on the deal to ensure everything was satisfactory. Make sure of satisfaction—and don't forget the little people. It's not always the people at the top who have influence.

Social skills

Do people enjoy your company? Do you enjoy the company of others? You'll get a lot more out of the negotiating process (and out of the opposition) if they like you. If you are basically shy or uncomfortable in a social situation, learn how to fix it.

This does not mean you should pretend to be enjoying yourself!

A genuine interest in others will help. Forget that you're dying inside—how do you know that quiet general manager across the room isn't suffering the same agonies? You don't have to be the life of the party. Cultivate a quiet, pleasant personality if this is more "you"—and be a good listener. Respond to what the other person says. Wear clothes that are appropriate for the occasion, but still "you"—you don't want to feel like a store dummy.

 If social skills are a problem, attend courses or read books on developing conversational skills or coping with shyness. Join a club like Toastmasters to learn how to think and talk "on your feet."

Self-control/teamwork

Negotiators who like to be one-person operators come unstuck more frequently than those who cooperate with others.

Teamwork means getting input from your team (and others in the company) at every stage. This includes groundwork, initial contact, and the big negotiation itself. You'll be able to exercise more self-control—an essential in negotiating—if you're taking into account not just what you want, but what the team wants. Best of all, you're spared that awful feeling of being all alone balancing on that tightrope.

 Think of your negotiation as a smoothly functioning machine, gears meshing soundlessly and effortlessly. You're only part of the whole; you can't work without the rest of the machine. Stand back and look at your "machine"

from a distance. What are all the little parts that need to work together to get the desired result? How can you make best use of resources?

Creativity

This separates the master negotiator from the overly talkative, inexperienced person. You should be constantly trying new things and expanding your skills. If you reach an impasse, there's usually a way around it. Can you trade off another part of the deal? Cut costs elsewhere? Throw in an added benefit from another part of the company or a related firm? If you go in with a "black-and-white-only" approach you'll find the negotiation tough going. There are infinite shades of gray.

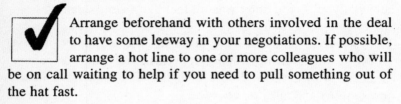 Arrange beforehand with others involved in the deal to have some leeway in your negotiations. If possible, arrange a hot line to one or more colleagues who will be on call waiting to help if you need to pull something out of the hat fast.

We are all quite different and seek different paths in life to satisfy our basic needs. Because of these differences, our behavior is normally a reflection of how those needs are to be satisfied. Moreover, needs in a long-drawn-out negotiation can change quite dramatically over the duration of the negotiating process.

Most psychologists regard the key to motivation as being those factors that empower behavior and give it some form of direction. It is also generally accepted that a motivated person or group in a negotiation will hang in there longer and harder than someone who is unmotivated or lacks competence through lack of training. You would do well, however, to keep in mind during negotiations that you cannot motivate the other side to a better deal. What you can do is create an atmosphere conducive to a favorable agreement. Playing a part in shaping conditions in this way will bring home to you what a dynamic process negotiation is.

Confident, adaptable negotiators are those who have prepared adequately, have the confidence to take calculated risks, and are ready to give the deal a fair go. In contrast, negotiators doomed from the start are those who have such a strong need for security that they will not commit themselves to the deal until the whole board of directors and every shareholder give the go-ahead.

Once you are able to separate the People component of the negotiation from the negotiation itself, you will find that problems tend to disappear. When you accept that the other side has the same needs and insecurities to satisfy that you have, you will be able to understand and rationalize their behavior.

So, what kinds of needs and insecurities are we talking about? People come to a negotiation with all kinds of needs, some of which may seem bizarre or incomprehensible to you. Here you are, seeking a good deal with the prospect of future transactions—and a reasonable profit—and all the other side seems to care about is being able to beat you down to nothing!

What makes them tick? Plenty of people in the past have sat down to analyze why people act the way they do. In brief, here are some of the needs that may be bugging your opponents:

The need to achieve

Most successful people have a high need to achieve—to do things of importance to them. This intense need helps to explain why some people commit what amounts to commercial suicide—"Close the deal at all costs."

They preplan negotiation with one thought paramount: to achieve what they set out to do. There is little room for compromise.

The need for challenge and responsibility

Some people feel a need for achievement within the negotiation itself. By providing challenge, achievement, and growth as the negotiation proceeds, you are satisfying their needs and are likely to come out of the proceedings with a satisfactory outcome for both sides.

The need to satisfy personal and company goals

Some negotiators are eager to accept responsibility when they can see how they and the company are working toward common goals. This consideration is vitally important when preparing for the negotiation. If you know that the other party feels this strongly about their product, service, or company, then the negotiation can move from an adversarial position to a problem-solving situation.

The need to be rewarded

No matter how sharp we are—or think we are—as negotiators, we all like to be given a pat on the back for something well done. The implications of this for negotiating are far-reaching:

> *People repeat behavior that is rewarded;*
> *they avoid behavior that is punished.*

At the negotiating table, the more initiatives from the other side that are rewarded, the greater the quality of options that will be generated. The underlying message here is to think carefully before rewarding or punishing a behavior pattern—it will affect the outcome of the negotiation.

What does it all mean?

The bottom line is this: you cannot motivate someone to do something, but you can create the conditions that will influence the other party to come to a favorable conclusion. This means that you are being truly persuasive, rather than being a manipulator in the negotiation.

Let's look at an example.

Suppose a company leaves a supplier alone in a small room for forty minutes prior to a negotiation.

What effect does this have?

It usually proves stressful for the person waiting. Doubts arise:

"They don't want the contract."

"They don't like me."

"I'm not important to them."

They are gaining an advantage by putting the other side in an unfriendly environment before the negotiating actually begins.

Consider this for a moment:

Just what does motivate you to get out of bed one morning, jump in a plane, and travel halfway around the world to commence a negotiation?

If your only answer is "Because the boss set it up," start worrying.

And start thinking.

To plan for a successful outcome to your negotiation, you must first know what really motivates you.

There are many more motivation models that could be discussed, but the main thrust of a discussion of any of them would require an understanding of your needs and what motivates you as a negotiator.

By knowing what motivates you, you can actually keep your emotions under control in any negotiation. A problem that often occurs in a negotiation is that logic can quickly disappear, letting emotions take over. Once this happens the negotiation is heading down a one-way street to disaster.

What can you do if you feel your control slipping while the negotiation is in progress?

Take a break.

At times, your emotional reaction will be exactly what the other side is aiming for. They're likely to have been trying a power tactic to make you lose your nerve.

As adults we are creatures of habit. We don't care much for any sort of change, but especially change involving pain. In a negotiation, we are likely to feel pain when the other side is pushing hard and we haven't planned adequately.

Let's face it:

If you don't know what motivates you as a negotiator,
you will lose.

If, however, you have clearly identified what you are trying to achieve, success is at least possible. Whoever has the greatest motivation in any negotiation is already way ahead.

CULTURAL NEGOTIATIONS

All over the world, businesspeople study the motivation and tactics of the Japanese.

Why do they appear so successful in negotiations both large and small?

Talent? Tenacity? Trickery?

Don't the same principles guide negotiating techniques in any country?

Aren't they motivated by the same things as anyone else?

Largely, yes.

In Japan, however, the knowledgeable negotiator can detect subtle differences in their approach to problem-solving.

It is wise to keep these differences in mind when dealing with the Japanese.

The differences mostly lie in the level of involvement and the approach to involvement between business and government.

Most Japanese people—particularly businesspeople—tend to be well-organized and have excellent internal communications.

There are other advantages, too, such as extensive networks of contacts and frequent consultation between Japanese officials and Japanese business houses.

This efficient and widespread level of consultation and mutual assistance has generated the concept of "Japan Inc." and provides a stark contrast to relationships between business and government in North America and Europe.

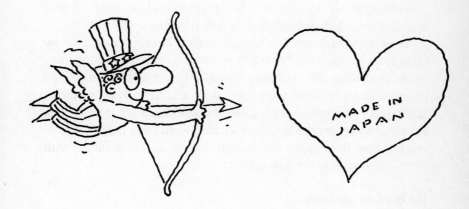

It can seem almost impossible for companies to compete with the motivation inherent in the "Japan Inc." ethos when they can't even get internal departments to cooperate. The ability of Japanese companies to cooperate in negotiations stands out in the arena of global negotiations. One example is in the area of supply of raw materials.

It is rare to see Japanese companies bid against each other. Companies from other countries will compete at times to the point of lunacy, tendering bottom-of-the-barrel prices just to get the business.

There are other innovative practices by the Japanese that we could do well to emulate, such as their quaintly named process of "parachuting down."

On retirement from government service, some officials may "parachute down" to a job in industry. Often such people hold staff appointments, but sometimes they will take line responsibility.

It is also common for certain senior businesspeople to be employed as special advisers in selected government situations. Such interaction and exchange lead to very close cooperation and understanding between the government and the private sector in Japan—not to mention the excellent communication it promotes. People are encouraged to stay motivated within any business dealing because this strong interaction fosters an environment that gives some margin for risk-taking.

The love-hate syndrome

At a recent conference, I was engaged in conversation with some senior executives when the conversation veered to Japanese trade practices.

"Unfair!" they all agreed.

Oh yes, they were prepared to admit that some of what the Japanese had achieved they had earned through hard work—but most of what they had to say was negative.

My interest piqued, I thought I'd investigate further.

Maybe these executives were dedicated to "buying American"?

I asked a couple of casual questions—and I'm sure their responses won't come as any surprise to you.

"What kind of cars do you drive?" I asked.

Almost all admitted to being the proud owner of a Japanese-made car. Their slightly self-conscious justification was along the lines of:

"It's just that they're better than most of the cars you can get locally."

Why?

They looked at me as though I should have known without having to ask. Their answers:

Better quality. Better price. Better image.

Better after-sales service . . . and so the list went on.

Better, better, better!

The story was much the same when I asked about other items in their homes: televisions, radios, electrical appliances. Most of them had bought Japanese products; again, mostly because of better quality.

The message that came through from this impromptu survey was clear.

Consumers, whether they live in North America, Australia, Europe, or Britain, love the Japanese. Or rather, they love the benefits that come with Japanese products.

Conversely, businesspeople who compete in the same markets hate the Japanese—because of their success.

All my research and experience over the past twenty years makes it obvious:

The Japanese view negotiation as a deadly serious business. Negotiations, to them, are a series of small battles in a great war. The war is economic: the battlefield is the world, and every time you negotiate with the Japanese you may be sure of one thing—to them, negotiation is not a game. It is critical that you keep this in mind when planning your next negotiation.

The amount of time and energy spent by the Japanese in preparing for any negotiation is truly awesome. Their attention to detail makes most other negotiators look weak by comparison.

RULES FOR NEGOTIATING WITH THE JAPANESE:

Respect the seriousness of their attitude toward the negotiation.

Prepare as though for battle: don't cut corners and don't underestimate the other side.

Arguably, the most competitive weapon of the Japanese is the nature of their government/business relationship, which allows them enormous flexibility in the way they compete internationally. Success in negotiation is virtually guaranteed when such flexibility is ranged against other world business/government structures.

Japan's trading partners have no comparable relationships. On the contrary—in most other countries, business and government waste a great deal of time fighting with each other.

One can well imagine the Japanese sitting back and watching all this with great satisfaction. As any military strategist knows, the best enemy to fight is already divided from within and going off in different directions. If negotiation is a battle, then the Japanese have a huge advantage.

Take a moment to reflect on the situation in the United States. Are business and government working with or against each other?

I'm fairly confident that I can accurately predict your response!

Of course, you can only do what is possible within the constraints of your own country's current situation. Just remember, your key to economic survival when negotiating with the Japanese is this: preparation, preparation, and more preparation!

The Japanese may not have all the answers, but they know how to use the total business and government network to succeed.

Their culture and heritage appear to have prepared them well for international and Pacific Rim negotiations.

There may not be a great deal you can do to change the way companies and government work together, but you can make sure you are very clear about your own and your company's motivations: you can work with your knowledge of what motivates you and what motivates others. In other words, you can give yourself the edge by learning about and practicing negotiation techniques at every opportunity, large or small.

Japan's greatest negotiation test will be dealing with a domestic and international market no longer in economic growth. They will have to adapt a new and creative approach to survive the downturn, especially with regard to their workers, who will no longer be guaranteed lifetime employment.

If you are uncomfortable or insecure, work on these things. Keep your ear to the ground for well-regarded courses at which you can add to your knowledge and hone your skills. Enthusiasm and commitment are great builders of motivation—and it will show in your results. Always consider the cultural differences in any negotiation. Don't assume that because something is okay at home that it will be the same overseas.

QUICK QUIZ

ARE YOU A MOTIVATED NEGOTIATOR?

Are you able to separate people from the negotiation?	yes	no
Do you have a clear understanding of your own motivations?	yes	no
Your attitude toward the negotiating process:		
Are you comfortable?	yes	no
Are you skilled?	yes	no
Are you frightened?	yes	no

Do you need to work on it?   yes   no

Do you know the difference between trying to motivate
someone to do something, and creating the conditions
that will influence a favorable conclusion?   yes   no

Do you have a clear knowledge of what motivates you
so that you can keep your emotions under control?   yes   no

Can you list five ingredients commonly found in a
successful negotiation by the Japanese?

     1. _____

     2. _____

     3. _____

     4. _____

     5. _____

Do you practice negotiation skills at any opportunity,
large or small?   yes   no

Do you keep up to date with current thinking and
writing on negotiation skills?   yes   no

Do you invest a lot of time in preparation?   yes   no

SCORING:

12 "yes" answers:	WORLD CLASS NEGOTIATOR!
10–11 "yes" answers:	Highly skilled negotiator
8–9 "yes" answers:	Hmm. Keep reading
6–7 "yes" answers:	Lots of practice needed
Less than 6 "yes" answers:	Are you sure you want to be a negotiator?

ANSWER to question on Japanese negotiations:

Five ingredients commonly found in a successful negotiation by the Japanese:

1. Cooperation
2. Organization
3. Excellent internal communication
4. Extensive network of contacts
5. Constant consultation between business and government

Chapter 3
The Negotiation Model

1% inspiration and 99% perspiration

—Thomas Edison

Remember how Columbus used superior negotiating skills to persuade Queen Isabella and King Ferdinand to fund his exploration of new trade routes? The nifty way he wangled honors and trade percentages?

Well, as impressive as that may have been, he didn't get that far by just making a wild guess at what would get the King and Queen on his side.

Initially, Columbus was stuck with the problem of how to approach the royal family with his ideas. After all, the good Queen's mind was currently absorbed by other problems. There was a war going on, and that was taking up large amounts of time and effort as well as large amounts of the country's money.

How, wondered Columbus, was he to kindle Queen Isabella's interest in the first place? He could imagine that the Queen, her mind occupied by other troubles, would not take kindly to an approach that seemed overly complicated or detailed. That way, chances of reaching an agreement were likely to fade, not improve.

So Columbus kept his ideas creative and his approach simple. (Come to think of it, Columbus probably invented the K.I.S.S. technique as well—Keep It Super Simple.) He knew that you don't come up with something appropriate without doing your homework. He set about quietly digging into the concerns that were uppermost in Queen Isabella's mind.

What did she need? Cash.

How could she get it? More trade.

Who could offer new trade routes? Christopher Columbus!

His approach to the whole negotiation process, from planning to completion, would probably have looked something like this:

It's effective, and it's simple.

THE NEGOTIATION MODEL

INVESTIGATIVE PHASE

PRESENTATION PHASE

BARGAINING PHASE

AGREEMENT PHASE

THE INVESTIGATIVE PHASE

It would not be too fanciful to say that the Investigative phase is where careers can be—and have been—made or destroyed. It is, without a doubt, the most important phase of the whole negotiation process.

It's easy to see why.

At this point, unless all relevant information about the negotiation is gathered, preparing for the negotiation is impossible.

After years of being involved in negotiations both big and small, I've learned to pick the FBTSOYP (fly-by-the-seat-of-your-pants) types on the other side. I'm always inwardly delighted when I spot them because I know that they are actually preparing for the negotiation as it takes place—and I also know it's 99 percent in the bag for me!

A saying I heard years ago has always remained with me, because I've found it to be very true:

Preparation compensates for lack of talent.

It's a good motto for you to remember, too. Do your homework. Find out what the other side needs, what they want, and what they can afford.

Like most negotiators, you probably feel that the hardest part is the Bargaining phase—but it is a fact that the tension of bargaining is greatly reduced if you're thoroughly prepared.

Once we are prepared, it's time for the Presentation phase to begin. In this phase we need to present our ideas to the other side in a logical manner, but based on information and facts gathered, not on emotion.

THE PRESENTATION PHASE

This is the fun part of the negotiation. It's creative. It's a challenge. You make your opening offer and add to it—and it's a chance to be so innovative that you can actually create an environment where the other side wants to do business.

(Just one thing: don't necessarily expect that this phase will be over in a morning's work . . . an opening offer in a deliberate negotiation may take years to be decided on!)

What do you have to look out for in the Presentation phase?

The good ol' number-one fear in the world: the fear of speaking before a group!

This nemesis crops up time and time again, either in the form of your own trembling limbs and pounding heart, or in the eyes and gestures of someone across the table. Many negotiators let their fear of public speaking get in the way of a good deal.

Negotiators from the other side are quick to pick up on nervousness from your body language. Jerky gestures, lack of eye contact, statements that fade at the end of the sentence—if these symptoms show up in your presentations, then again, look around for courses or speakers' clubs, such as Toastmasters, to combat the problem.

Meanwhile, in this Presentation phase, thorough preparation will aid you more than anything else. You will find nervousness declines in proportion to the amount of preparation you've done. It's easier to speak persuasively with all the facts at your fingertips.

If you have prepared conscientiously and know your material, the most important thing you can do is to maintain a positive attitude. Assuming that the other side is genuine in their desire to do business, an effective presentation will allow you to move smoothly into the Bargaining phase.

THE BARGAINING PHASE

This is the phase where stomachs knot up, knuckles whiten, and people breathe harder. The fight or flight syndrome takes over! Emotions run wild. People may yell, scream, or walk out of the negotiation.

Don't you! *Stay in control.*

The negotiator's tools are discipline and control.

Strangely enough, this phase really allows the whole deal to take on a feeling of legitimacy. After all, you've keyed yourself up for this. Think about it for a moment: if you were to walk into a room and make an opening offer and it was accepted, what would your reaction be?

Be honest, now! You would feel a tiny bit flat, wouldn't you? You'd probably feel almost cheated—your reasoning would say: "I could have got a better deal!"

In the Bargaining phase, you need to give careful consideration to the style you will use.

Most Western cultures dislike the concept of bargaining or haggling, but, when using the Quick style of negotiating, you need to be a good bargainer to be successful. The Deliberate style is different, although haggling is still occasionally necessary. Whichever method you use, make your watchwords discipline and control. It is important that we leave our egos at home and concentrate on the most creative way to seek agreement with the other side.

Watch for the experienced negotiators who play the power tactics game. They know that this is the time to push for a slightly better deal. In effect, what they say to the other side is something like: "Okay, you've got a good deal going here. How about a little extra. . . ?"

Usually the other side is reluctant to lose what they have gained, so they'll agree to small concessions to save negotiating again. On small deals it often appears trivial, but on bigger deals the expenses can mount up.

If a group uses these tactics against you, make a mental note to remember it if you negotiate with them again. You'll be ready for them to leave their best options to be discussed and negotiated toward the end—just before the Agreement phase.

THE AGREEMENT PHASE

Here we are at last—ready for all the final details of the deal to be put together and wrapped up. But don't let your guard down—it's not over yet. Even though this may appear to be the area where everyone can settle down, it's not.

Both sides need to feel that

All points along the way have been recorded correctly, and

All points are agreed upon within the context of the negotiation.

Probably the biggest decision that needs to be made at this point is where the final agreement will take place. All sorts of political reasons within the negotiation may dictate where this will occur—in fact, the place of the final agreement may become a major issue to be negotiated. If that's the case, use it as a means of gaining or giving a final concession. Make it work for you, not against everything you have achieved.

Needs and motivation in the different phases

As discussed in chapter 2, it is imperative to decide in detail the needs to have fulfilled by going into the negotiation:

Are the needs totally organizational, or personal, or a combination of the two?

In the Investigative phase, your individual needs are low. Your real concern is that of the organization, as you are only gathering and sorting through all available information.

In the Presentation phase, your needs are very high and the organization's needs are low. Yours are high because you're the one standing there trying to stay cool and collected before a group while delivering a formal presentation!

During the Bargaining phase, both your needs and the organizational needs are high, because the critical factors of the negotiation are open for discussion.

Finally, during the Agreement phase of the negotiation, the needs of the organization are high, but your individual needs are low. You're coming down off that tension-induced high; there is a feeling that the hard work has been done during the Bargaining phase and it's only the organizational needs that are important in the agreement process.

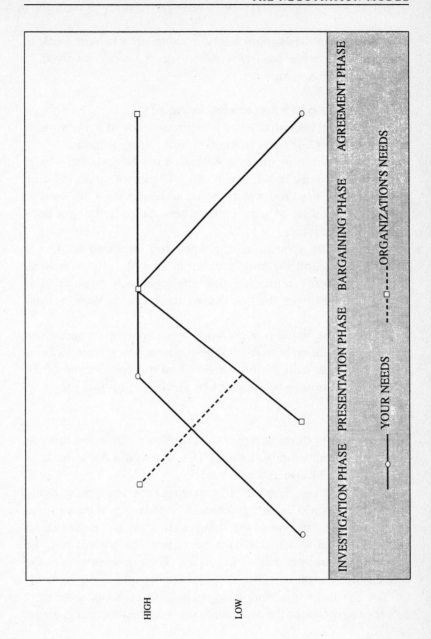

Be aware of what motivates you to do all the hard work in preparing and what motivates you to do the work involved in reaching an agreement.

How does this tie in with the Columbus Technique?

Cast your mind back to chapter 1, where we looked at the various features of the Quick and Deliberate styles of negotiation.

The knowledge of the four phases of the Negotiation Model that we've just looked at is an integral part of understanding which style to use. You will find that all four phases are used in the Deliberate style of negotiation when you're building a partnership for the future.

However, the opposite is true when you are using the Quick style. You may find anything from one to all of the phases present.

You need only remember that although each negotiation is totally different from the one before, the basic elements remain the same.

To make the whole process work, it is important to appreciate that the negotiation starts from the moment you decide to enter into the process with someone else. I find it helps to think of the whole negotiation as being a bit like playing a part in a play.

A play?

Yes, a play.

When you perform in a play, you take on a role—and this can be useful to today's negotiator. In fact, you could do worse than adopt Mickey Mouse as a role model.

Not so long ago, I had the illuminating experience of studying at the Disneyworld Training Center in Florida. It was educational in many ways, but one of the things that made the most impact was the way in which staff members threw themselves into the role of the characters they were playing. Their commitment to the role ensured success.

You can make this work for you, too. If you adopt a different role for each phase of the negotiation process, then success is yours.

This does not mean, of course, that you start acting like someone with four different personalities and have the other side phoning for a straitjacket. It means you view each phase as being dependent on the others, but requiring different skills.

The more effort you put into each role, the easier you will find the negotiating process.

What do I mean, then, by adopting different roles?

First, you become a Detective.

This, naturally enough, is for the Investigative phase. You need to be more gimlet-eyed than Columbo, more persistent than Sam Spade. Find out, in short, every possible piece of information you can about the negotiation.

Investigate the background, just as Columbus did when planning his strategy with Queen Isabella. Clearly identify the people involved, both internally and externally. What resources and data do you need to make a decision?

Then you change hats.

You're in the Presentation phase now, so think like a Lawyer.

You've done the spadework. Now you need to be able to present the other side's case better than they can! Once you can do that, then you have prepared your case—because you, like a good lawyer, will be in a position to predict the other side's objections before they open their mouths.

What's next?

The Bargaining phase—and with it, a step up the social scale for you! Now you're going to become a Judge.

What do good judges do? Well, they always listen attentively to all of the information being presented before making a decision, don't they? What's more, a judge knows that occasionally a negotiator will become emotional and distort the facts. By wearing your judge's hat (or wig) you can emotionally keep your distance, being aware that sometimes the other party may become emotional just to gain an advantage. Make a decision only when you have listened to all of their facts and demands, not before.

Finally you shed your judge's robes and make the transition to a lynx-eyed Accountant for the Agreement phase.

What's the role of the accountant?

Accountants check everything carefully, being alert for inconsistencies. The temptation in this Agreement phase is to heave a sigh of relief and think: "Thank goodness the haggling is over!" and relax.

No, no. No relaxing yet.

Check those facts and figures.

This is where a lot of "add-ons" occur in the negotiation.

Never allow the last word to come via any verbal agreements: ears, it has been said, have lousy memories. Sad but true.

ROLE SUMMARY

If you develop the habit of adopting different roles for each phase of the negotiation, you will quickly notice how easily you are handling each successive stage. Your confidence in the roles you are playing will communicate itself not only to the opposition, but also to your own team. Success, you will find, will come more easily.

Just ask the employees of Disneyworld, Florida, who know not only why 25 million guests visit each year, but why people keep coming back. They love the experience, and they know that Mickey Mouse and Donald Duck will always be playing their part.

Are you thinking (somewhat *testily*): "I'm no Donald Duck. I'm no actor, either. How am I expected to learn how to do this?"

Don't try to be too analytical about it. The real secret in using the different roles in different phases is this: just get started. Forget about any limiting thoughts you may have—just do it. As Zig Ziglar often says: "Too much analysis causes paralysis!"

In brief:

ROLE	PHASE	CHARACTERISTICS
Detective	Investigative	– Information Gathering – Internal/External
Lawyer	Presentation	– Prepare their case – Present your case
Judge	Bargaining	– Listen to other side – Look for options
Accountant	Agreement	– Place of agreement – Check everything

These roles can be used

internally (when negotiating for the support of a project), or
externally (when negotiating with the country you've been working with for the past ten years).

The further you delve into this business of negotiating, the more interesting and challenging it becomes. Role-playing is not only a challenge to your creativity, but actually fun once you've mastered it. It can also be one of the ways to overcome your reluctance in regard to public speaking. This sounds like a contradiction, I know, but it's true.

Classroom studies have shown a curious development with shy children—if they can "pretend" to be someone else (for instance, using puppets) their shyness actually disappears. Although in reality low self-confidence refuses to allow the child to be articulate or persuasive, if they are asked to play a role the ego seems to say: "Oh, all right, the person you're pretending to be could probably do that"—and the child's whole personality changes!

One of the greatest benefits of role-playing is being able to distance yourself from the emotional traps. With experience, it will become clear to you that the negotiators who keep their cool are more likely to achieve the outcome they want.

Let's look at your own experiences.

You can probably remember occasions when negotiations went well for you and other times when you just wanted to crawl under the nearest rock.

Cast your mind back in time to the last negotiation that left you feeling dejected with the results. How do you think this came about? Were you forced to just take it on the chin when someone launched an attack (because you had no comeback)? Did you get caught when you snapped unthinkingly at a bait dangled by the opposition?

Hmmmm. Food for thought.

Now think about the most recent successful negotiation. How much did that happy outcome have to do with your being well-prepared? How much did it have to do with the fact that you knew the emotional attacks were launched at the presentation, not at you?

If you are the target of an attack, imagine it as being like someone passing you a ticking package. Smile at them—and pass it right back!

Remember, each negotiation is unique. By planning and using the Negotiation Model, by implementing these simple steps, you will develop skills few people possess. It's hard work, but the outcomes are worth it.

SUMMARY

1. These are the keys to success:

   Creative utilization of the Negotiation Model used by Columbus

   Ensuring you understand the method, and follow these four phases in the negotiation:

   - Investigative
   - Presentation
   - Bargaining
   - Agreement

2. Use role-playing to develop a suitable approach to each phase:

   When in the Investigative phase, become a Detective.

   When in the Presentation phase, become a Lawyer.

   When in the Bargaining phase, become a Judge.

   When in the Agreement phase, become an Accountant.

Chapter 4

The Investigative Phase

If you know the enemy and know yourself, you need not fear the result of a hundred battles.

—Sun Tzu, *The Art of War* (500 B.C.)

Time after time, I've been called in to consult on negotiations when things started going sour. Panic sets in. The negotiators, sometimes with huge amounts of money or vital contracts at stake, are casting wildly around for help.

I know what I'm going to find before I even walk in.

Simple lack of preparation.

Usually, the negotiators concerned had raced into the deal as quickly as they could, afire with enthusiasm (and, quite often, the killer instinct working overtime).

But how much time had they spent preparing? Anything from a few hours (I kid you not) to a week.

I start asking questions.

I ask about their knowledge of current competitive prices.

I ask how they arrived at the style and strategy they eventually ended up using.

I ask what fallback positions they had planned.

That's just for starters. It doesn't take long for people to start shuffling feet and avoiding my eye.

Here is a copy of the checklist I ask them to use.

In their preparation for this negotiation, did they:

PREPARATION	YES	NO
make sure they would have ongoing support from the internal environment (the organization)?		
thoroughly research prices?		
consider the effect of the external environment on the negotiation (i.e., the world economy, acts of war, etc.)?		
take into account the long-term corporate goals of the organization?		
(if appropriate) consult with unions?		
take into account political policies that might impact on the negotiation?		
plan fallback positions?		
take into account their own needs and motivations?		
try to predict as many objections that might be raised as possible?		
determine ahead of time the style and strategy that were likely to be appropriate?		

When I ask these questions, most of these people clamoring for help look at me blankly.

Internal and external environments?

Style and strategy?

Needs and motivations?

Why, no. They just knew what they wanted and went after it—well, yeah, they had a few tricks up their sleeves, of course. Knew a few tactics.

"So what went wrong?" I ask.

They don't know. Or:

The other side used stalling tactics.

The other side used dirty tricks.

Or it was the company's fault: "You know how it is, the right hand doesn't know what the left is doing . . ."

Yes, I know how it is.

They should have known "how it is," too.

You never go into a negotiation without knowing how much support you'll get from all sections of your company.

You never say: "This is our approach. If it fails, it fails."

Always leave room to maneuver.

The new elements for negotiation in the late 1990's and into the next century are:

1. Prepare
2. Prepare
3. Prepare

Before the negotiation actually begins, you must gather as much information as possible.

Remember: the more pain you experience in preparation, the less pain there'll be in the Bargaining phase. If you're thoroughly prepared, you'll have room to be more creative when bargaining.

Unprepared people tend to be far more positional in their stance. If you're unprepared; if you don't have a planning sheet, when things get sticky—what happens? The adrenalin starts to flow and you fall back to good ol' "fight or flight."

It's either: "I've got to win" or "I've got to run."

No compromise.

No real success, either.

The aim of the Investigative phase is to gather information. You must enter the negotiation prepared for the journey. You need to think carefully about how both the internal (workplace) and external environments will affect the negotiation.

Do you know the strengths of your organization? Do you know its weaknesses? If you don't, then set about finding out. You cannot develop workable plans otherwise. Most advice on negotiations concentrates on the minefields outside the company, but you need to remember that for the novice negotiator there is often more danger from the internal political realities.

THE INTERNAL ENVIRONMENT

Formal structure

Four questions you need to consider:

1. How many levels of management within your organization do you need to deal with to have a decision ratified and implemented?
2. If you come from a sales environment: how quickly can the stock be put into inventory?
3. If you are working for an international company: do the goods have to come from another market or even another country?
4. If you have to discount the goods, and the accounting department calculates that the deal will cost the company money: who has to okay it? how will they handle it?

The formal structure of the organization will really dictate the amount of preparation needed in the negotiation.

It is important to ensure that every department affected by your deal has a degree of input during the Investigative phase of the negotiation.

The reasons for this are obvious:

We are all more committed to an outcome if we have some input or degree of control.

You run the risk of missing some vital information if you don't, thus alienating not only the other side, but those with whom you work.

Informal structure

Everybody knows that the person with the title is not necessarily the person with the power.

If you want to be successful in your negotiations, you must know the informal structure of the company.

It's not something you'll find documented for you anywhere. It's up to you to know "who's who in the zoo" so that you can get all the necessary information quickly to prepare for the negotiation. The informal structure of any organization is very powerful. Use it for information-gathering, then prepare and deliver the best in your negotiation.

Corporate goals

If you belong to a large organization, then you must understand clearly what the long-term strategic goals of the organization mean to your negotiation.

Beware of accepting a vague corporate statement like:

"Just go out there and get the best deal you can!"

You're likely to find that what you think is good, the finance director will consider a disaster. Who needs to return to the company to be treated like a leper, after honestly doing the best you could?

This does not mean you shouldn't take risks in your career, but it does mean you should cover your tail. So, in the investigative phase, do this:

Start running some "What if. . . ?" scenarios on different outcomes and make sure your solutions tie in with corporate goals.

Departmental relationships

Most organizations nowadays are operating under a far flatter structure than they did ten years ago. This brings problems in its wake, as most of the key positions are held by executives who have enormous demands on their time. This can create problems when you need the cooperation of such an executive to get a number of departments working together on one deal.

Let's look at a possible scenario:

You have two weeks to prepare your case before you fly to London. The purpose: you need to renegotiate an old supply contract and open a new agreement on some computer hardware.

Internally, you need to:

Discuss the finance position (e.g., the dollar is dropping)

Know if the technical specifications will fit the local market

Discuss the fact that the warehouse is already full of other products that aren't selling

Meanwhile, marketing has told you that this new product is a "hot one"; no one has time for a meeting with the other departments and your career is on the line.

Welcome to reality!

Here's where it's essential to know your informal power structure. Know the hierarchy and power politics in your own organization—not only to give you the edge in a negotiation, but also to protect yourself.

Personal relationships

Isn't it always the way that when you need something done in a hurry, the person from whom you most need cooperation is the one who likes you about as much as they like a toothache? The same truth applies to both internal relationships and external (customer) relationships.

You need to be building relationships all the time.

You've all seen those movies and TV shows that depict the successful executive as some kind of hard-bitten caricature. You know, "He's a hard man and drives his staff hard too—but no one can nail a deal like he can!"

This image is one of Hollywood's most successful lies.

A more accurate picture of a successful executive (although, of course, not one nearly as dramatic or interesting to viewers) is someone who is able to build relationships internally. This type of person is usually able to build trust at the start of the negotiation and maintain that trust throughout all the proceedings.

Unions

If the deal will impact in any way with the union members—do your homework first. Otherwise there is a high possibility that you will find yourself over that well-known barrel.

Plan before, not after, the event.

To summarize:

The internal environment, with its various subsets, must be in order if you are to succeed in the external environment.

You must know

the formal structure,

the informal structure,

corporate goals,

departmental relationships,

personal relationships, and

the extent of union involvement.

If you can survive the minefield of the internal environment, the next major obstacle is the external arena.

THE EXTERNAL ENVIRONMENT

International marketplace

Welcome to complexity! Here you have not only the uniqueness of different markets and differences in language and culture, but a myriad of other issues. Those issues apply equally to your domestic market.

Just look at the way many countries approached international competition in the late 1970s. Most of the industrialized world was looking at moving into the high-tech area. Then the late 1980s saw the pendulum swing back again into the primary industries.

At this stage in the 1990s, most are looking at the concept of how to add value to those products, prior to exporting.

You don't need to be an economist to see that we have a problem with our negative balance of payments. Negotiators from other countries naturally take this into account in their negotiations. Make sure that when you negotiate in international markets, you know the value of the other country's trade balance or imbalance. This will greatly affect your perceived outcome.

Political and economic policies

What is the current political situation of the group with whom you are about to negotiate? Within your own national boundaries this does not cause a great problem, but what about your neighbors?

If your product or service is remotely related to defense issues, are you aware of what effect a coup (for example) in one of your foreign markets would have on your business? It's essential that you take such possibilities (even if remote) into account.

As for economic forces, a quick look at history will show the massive changes in our financial markets as the value of the dollar has risen and fallen, and the way interest rates have soared and subsided over the last few decades. You must be prepared for this sort of activity so your firm won't go under.

Check your contracts.

If you have a contract with an international firm, does your agreement allow for changes to be made for exchange-rate fluctuations? Has the finance director made you create a back-down clause for a movement in the currency?

If you are a small business owner, can you obtain an international license? This may give you a competitive edge, but what will it cost you in the negotiation?

Geographic location

Look carefully at the location of the market compared to your distribution outlets. Maybe you are located in New York, but you have to deliver to Hong Kong. What type of penalty do you think the other side will impose for late delivery?

Can you negotiate part assembly in New York and then, say, subassembly at the point of delivery? How will the time constraints of traveling to distant locations affect your ability to negotiate? If you have a long flight, allow time to rest. If you know it's going to be a tough negotiation, fly in a couple of days ahead of schedule.

Information age

How does the "Age of Information" affect your negotiation? It means that you have to prepare, then keep preparing. Once you have done that, start again. Those facing you on the other side of the negotiating table will not leave a stone unturned. Every last dollar and cent will be checked.

The resources available to all corporations means that information concerning your deal can be loaded onto a system and checked in minutes.

There is a positive side to all this, of course. If you need to access information from anywhere in the world, you too can do it almost instantly.

PLANNING

The problem with most of our training concerning planning is that people tend to think real events should march happily in step with all the details included in their plans. How often have you seen that happen?

The first step in becoming a great negotiator is to know that all plans become only a guide to our actions and decisions—they are not the ultimate destination.

Flexibility is the key.

We must be creative with our own options in planning and also be aware of creative solutions the other side may offer as a means of reaching an agreement.

If anyone in your team suggests that a particular point is not negotiable, start to question that stand. Do the same with your own attitudes. Taking a stubborn stance may create an impasse during the Bargaining phase of the negotiation.

Here I will detail a Planning Model that has been successful for many negotiators. It will be successful for you, too. The more you use it the more creative you will become in your negotiations.

Why do I suggest a model? The main benefit is that you will be able to spend less time in planning for the negotiation, as you will be using the same planning approach or structure on each subsequent negotiation. Each negotiation will have many issues and conflicts to be resolved; the model will focus your thinking and preparation.

There are normally four main issues to be decided upon to reach an agreement. Price, though obviously always one of the four main issues, is not the only factor in commercial negotiations. (It may not even be the main issue if you're looking at an ongoing relationship.)

Knowing that there are four main issues makes it easier to work through the planning process. To start the ball rolling, the issues for consideration will revolve around our perceived outcomes. (Remember those?)

OUTCOMES

As discussed in earlier chapters, the three options that you will work through are the Realistic, the Acceptable, and the Worst Possible outcome.

It means that before you do anything else you are already asking yourself this one valuable question:

"Why am I negotiating with the other side?"

Once you can answer that question you are already focusing on your motivation to negotiate. The rest is easy.

Say, for example, you are looking to buy a new house for your family. You see an advertisement in the paper for a house in the area that you like and it is in your price range. The house unfortunately is not being sold by an agent, it is being sold by the owner and is advertised for $500,000 "or best offer"—so you know they are prepared to move on price.

Already one of the four issues has a number of options.

You visit the property. Excited, you all decide this is the house for the family.

You start on the Investigative phase and find out that similar properties in the area have sold for an average selling price of around $430,000. Being a good Detective you also know that properties with a view of the river will command an extra $20,000 or a little bit more. You can now start the planning process of determining the options that you have for the price outcome of the negotiation.

Realistic outcome	$430,000
Acceptable outcome	$450,000
Worst Possible outcome	$500,000

But let's not make it too easy. Let's say the owner of the house is a good negotiator and has started to plan the outcomes. The options for the owner would look like this:

Realistic outcome	$500,000
Acceptable outcome	$475,000
Worst Possible outcome	$430,000

You might say at this stage that there is at least a $70,000 difference between the buyer and the seller. Remember our definition for the negotiation process. This is where you start to use creative options to resolve the difference. I refer to this as the Rule of Four. My research shows that most negotiations are ultimately decided by dealing with four main issues. By looking at four major issues per negotiation instead of just one (price), you are allowing yourself creative ways to get the best deal possible. If you are buying the house from the owner and not through an agent, the four issues you might decide upon could be:

1. Price
2. Possession date
3. Terms for payment
4. Accessories in the home

You've already worked through issue number 1 (price), deciding upon the Realistic, Acceptable, and Worst Possible outcomes.

Now it's time to do the same with issues 2, 3, and 4. You would then have enough different options to be able to achieve an agreement suitable to both sides.

The same process can be accomplished whether you are negotiating for a new supply agreement, an audit or a consulting contract, an overdue salary increase, or even buying a car.

Decide on the four issues that are important to you and work through each one for the different outcomes. I can assure you that you'll then find the Presentation and the Bargaining phases that much easier.

Research

Once you have gathered all the information you need, it's time to start running through different scenarios with all those facts.

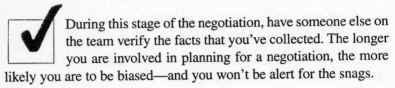 During this stage of the negotiation, have someone else on the team verify the facts that you've collected. The longer you are involved in planning for a negotiation, the more likely you are to be biased—and you won't be alert for the snags.

Regardless of the complexity of the negotiation, it helps if you have devised a simple spreadsheet that will allow the different outcomes to be calculated at the drop of a hat. You need to be aware that during the whole negotiation, the facts and figures will change.

Flexibility is essential during the process, so you can alter your thinking if new information becomes available.

Define

The next step is to define the objections that will be raised to your proposal during the negotiation. Also, decide upon the different positions that will be adopted during the process. At this point the easiest way to work out any objections that will be raised during the negotiation is to simply put yourself in the shoes of the other side.

Let's go back to our $500,000 house-buying example for a moment. Imagine if I were the buyer and walked into this negotiation to start the proceedings with something like this:

> *"Your house should suit our needs pretty well.*
> *I'll give you $380,000 for it."*

By projecting myself into the mind of the seller, I think it's fairly safe to predict that I would probably be running for the door with the family dog snapping at my heels within five seconds.

Don't insult the intelligence of the other party—an unrealistic beginning will set the other side against you from the start.

Determine

Now it's time to determine

(a) the style you will use in the negotiation; and

(b) the strategy you will adopt for a mutually satisfying agreement for both parties.

Remember our discussions on style in the opening chapters? You are now at the point where you need to decide on the style for this negotiation.

Quick or Deliberate?

As an example, let's imagine that Sally Trainer, a consultant, is working with an organization with the aim of developing a training plan and providing training services. The main question Sally should be asking is

"Do I want more business with this company?"

If the answer is yes, a Deliberate style would be appropriate.

If it's no, then Sally should be looking at the Quick style, which is more appropriate for a one-time sale.

Okay. Sally has now decided she's not keen on an ongoing relationship with TopNotch Products, Inc.; this once will be enough, thanks. The decision is for a Quick style negotiation, and Sally should adopt a strong positional stand over the major issue—price. She should reason that the price should be as high as possible, even slightly inflated. After all, there'll be no return performance.

What if Sally had decided that TopNotch Products would be a good source for her relationship-building business (not to mention a bit of a cash flow) for some time? In this case, Sally could see a reason for adopting a deliberate approach and using many issues in the negotiation. Agreement could be reached by using a problem-solving approach.

At our training seminars, people often ask questions like:

"What tactics should we use to get the business?"

"Should we trick them with false information or a false promise?"

"Just say we're discussing quantities, discounts, stuff like that—couldn't I sort of hint at a big order just around the corner?"

I'm not comfortable with that sort of game-playing or use of trickery. In the long run I don't think it gets you very far or does your business much good. Your fairest price for a one-time order should always be given in the initial proposal.

In fact, what works for me is somewhat different from advice given in many current books on negotiating. My answer to questions about tactics is usually "use no tactics at all."

If you have:

prepared in detail,

worked through the various outcomes, and

worked through the four main issues,

then there's no need for "tactics."

"Tactics" too often seem to smack of skullduggery. They create tension and destroy trust. They tend to be used by negotiators who work from the "quick fix" positional style of logic. Your only tactic should be to walk away if it's not worth continuing.

Review approaches

Finally, the last phase before mapping out your approach to the negotiation is to review approaches and appoint a Consequence Thinker.

Reviewing your approach to the process allows you to think critically through all the assumptions you have made. Step by step, you need to think through all the decisions you have made concerning the internal or external environment, right through to the style you will adopt for the negotiation.

If the negotiation is important, and it is a Deliberate style that you are adopting, then once you have reviewed all the information you are in a position to find a Consequence Thinker.

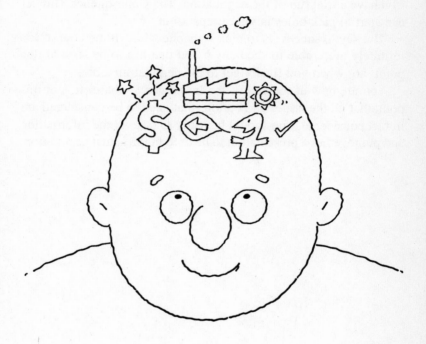

The role of the Consequence Thinker is to wear the shoes of the other side. This person should be fully acquainted with all the facts and information surrounding the other side's viewpoint. The person should be chosen for their ability to think objectively, because at this stage you have become totally subjective in your thinking.

The benefits to you are obvious:

You have a trial run of the negotiation. The Consequence Thinker can start to pick holes in your preparation.

The key to success is to pick someone who will be honest. It's infinitely preferable to shed any blood that has to be shed at this point, not when you finally get to the negotiating table.

You are now at the end of the Investigative phase. It is at this point that all the issues and options that need to be considered are in fact considered. You should be ready to take all the information and put together a presentation to be used in the actual negotiation.

SUMMARY

1. The three P's of the 1990s: Prepare, Prepare, Prepare!

2. The purpose of the Investigative phase is to gather information so you are prepared for the journey ahead.

3. Knowledge of the internal environment is essential. Know:

The formal structure
- levels of management
- movement of stock
- international supply lines
- who authorizes discounts

The informal structure
- who's who at the zoo
- who wields the "real" power?

Corporate goals

Departmental relationships
- possible communication problems
- hierarchy and power politics

Personal relationships
- be building relationships all the time
- establish trust

Unions
- if they're involved, consult

4.   Know the external environment:

The international marketplace
- primary versus secondary industries
- added value to goods or services
- balance of payments

Political and economic policies
- defense issues
- interest and exchange rates

Geographic location
- market location versus distribution outlets
- effects of jet lag

The Information Age
- facts can be instantly checked

5.   Plan your journey:
Plans are a guide, not our ultimate destination
Flexibility is the key
Use a planning model

6.   Work through possible outcomes:
Three options: Realistic, Acceptable, Worst Possible
Why am I negotiating?
Creative options: work on four major issues

7. Needs and motivation:

    Are your needs organizational, personal, or a combination?

    Look ahead: investigate your needs and motivation in each phase of the negotiation

8. Research:

    Have someone else verify the facts

    Be flexible: adapt your thinking to new information

9. Define objections:

    Predict objections

    Decide own positions

10. Determine style and strategy:

    Do I want more business from this client?

11. Review approaches:

    Last phase: appoint a "Consequence Thinker"

Chapter 5

The Presentation Phase

To tell the truth, I hate public speaking!

—Harrison Ford

When even stars like Harrison Ford admit they hate speaking before a group, it gives some comfort to the rest of us. After all, there are not too many of us who react with pleasure at the prospect of public speaking.

Why are so many people terrified when it comes to public speaking?

If we can express ourselves in a confident and articulate manner in front of a small number of our colleagues, why can't we do the same before a group of strangers?

Part of it, I guess, is that our friends and colleagues will put up with a few bloopers. They'll offer friendly suggestions, or put in timely warnings about something we may have overlooked:

"Hey, Greg, you haven't really backed up your claims about our product being better than any other on the market. How about throwing in a few statistics?"

With friends, it's also less likely that we'll react with embarrassment or anger when we've messed up. It's usually:

"Phew, good thing you picked that one up!"

So how can we transfer the confidence we show with friends to the "stage" of the negotiation arena? How can we stop the fear of public speaking from interfering with the presentation of our proposal during a negotiation?

This fear can be so knee-weakening, so mind-numbing, that it actually affects the way we present our information. Painfully aware of the effect we're having on those listening, our attention is diverted to our nervousness instead of the presentation.

I've mentioned in earlier chapters that the best cure for nervousness is thorough preparation. This is the key not only to achieving success in the negotiation overall, but in conquering that awful blanketing fear ("oh no . . . all-eyes-are-on-me") in the Presentation phase.

So here, in a few easy steps, is the solution to your problem:

Adopt the role of a good defense lawyer.

Prepare the other side's case.

Present the reasons for your case being better.

Abraham Lincoln was one person who used this process to great effect when presenting his defense cases in court.

Let's make things even easier, by looking at the two major considerations for your Presentation phase.

1. Map out the negotiating Planning Sheet.
2. Make the presentation to the other side.

Sounds simple, doesn't it? Perhaps too simple?

Relax. All the best methods are! All you're doing is learning to carefully prepare the pros and cons for both sides. It's more fun than Rubik's Cube, Scrabble, and cryptic crosswords all put together, and easier than any of them—and way easier than standing there in the middle of a presentation quivering like jelly from fear.

So, first you develop your side's Planning Sheet for the nego-tiation—then you become a double agent:

Put on your trenchcoat and black hat and, chortling nastily, prepare the other side's presentation, too.

Cover every possible contingency you can think of. It will help save you from being confronted with sudden surprises dur-ing the negotiation. (It might give them a few unpleasant surpris-es instead, when they realize you've got an answer for everything they throw at you.)

Once you can present their case as effectively as your own, you are ready to go.

What other benefits are there to doing this extra planning? For a start, you'll be prepared for emotional outbursts and appeals by the other side during the negotiation. ("Oh yeah," you'll think as they start spluttering indignantly, "I thought they might get a bit upset about this . . .")

Stay calm. You're doing fine.

THE PLANNING SHEET

The Planning Sheet is the tool to be used in streamlining all the available information into the "must-know" data and information for your presentation. At this point, all the hard work involved in the Investigative phase is realized. In front of you will be pages of satisfying information on the issues you've already discussed with your team. All you have to do now is map them out as points to be used in the presentation.

By using the negotiating Planning Sheet, you are making sure that all the information you will need in the Presentation phase is there at your fingertips in a useful format. In your planning you need only the keywords for your preparation—you can go ahead and explain them in detail during the presentation.

 Don't get carried away and bury the other side in an avalanche of information. (Some negotiators do this to impress the other side with the amount of research they've done.)

Don't do it.

Instead of being overawed by your efficiency, they're far more likely to be

(a) bored, and

(b) resentful.

An excess of information leads to a tendency for the presenter to waffle or unwittingly give away too much information to the opposition. The Planning Sheet will help steer you away from these pitfalls. Use it to identify your critical information, and present nothing else!

To demonstrate the usefulness of the sheet, I will work through one of the examples looked at in the last chapter.

If you remember, we were looking at buying a house from a "For Sale by Owner." If it's been a while since you read the last chapter, look back for a moment to refresh your memory.

The four issues identified were:

1. Price

2. Possession date

3. Terms for payment

4. Accessories in the home

Let's have a look at how I would fill out the Planning Sheet. First of all, my style would be closer to the quick end of the continuum rather than the deliberate. How did I work this out? Well, we have identified the need to establish trust to commence the negotiation, but I also know that our chances of negotiating again with those home owners are probably slim. Having established the style, I would start to prepare all four issues. Price would be number 1, and it would look like this:

Realistic	$425,000
Acceptable	$450,000
Worst Possible outcome	$480,000

I would then continue with the other three options, working through each outcome until the Planning Sheet was completed.

If you doubt the power of the sheet, just quickly look at how many different options you have covered by using the approach based on four issues and three different outcomes.

It's so powerful that I guarantee when you use it once, you will never go back to the old "shoot-from-the-hip" approach to negotiating. Wyatt Earp is dead.

"Wait a minute," I can hear someone out there saying. "It's nowhere near that simple in the kind of negotiations I have to do. My company negotiates supply agreements with a whole heap of different suppliers—and even then it's for a range of goods and services, not just one item."

Okay. I understand those problems; in my company we do a lot of training for organizations with just those needs. And you're right.

In preparing the Planning Sheet, you'd need a somewhat different approach to selecting the style, the outcomes, and the four issues involved in the negotiation.

For starters, the style selected would be at the deliberate end of the continuum, as a high level of trust and an established business relationship would need to exist.

Then we have the four issues. In this situation (broadly speaking) the four issues might look like this:

TERMS

PRICE

DELIVERY

QUANTITY

NEGOTIATION PLANNING SHEET

Who is involved?

Describe the current situation

Style: Quick/Deliberate – why?

Describe the resources needed to complete the negotiation

Issues	Outcomes		
	Realistic	Acceptable	Worst Possible
1.			
2.			
3.			
4.			

Suppose we now look at terms. The sheet would look like this:

Realistic	90 Days
Acceptable	60 Days
Worst Possible	30 Days

From here on, it's the same as the last example. You work through the remaining three issues, deciding the various outcomes for each.

Once the Planning Sheet has been completed, you are in a position again to review all the information you have gathered and are now ready to prepare for the Presentation phase of the negotiation.

PRESENTATION PHASE

Each phase of the negotiation is important. However, this part of the negotiation is where you have an opportunity to show the other side that you are serious and, in fact, prepared to commence the negotiation. Now, communication skills are the key component to being successful in any presentation. Regrettably, there are lots of people out there who neglect these basic skills because "everybody knows how to communicate."

Take a moment here, before you read on, to jot down what you think communication is.

Talking?

Listening?

Vocabulary skills?

Communication is more than that. It includes all the things we do in our presentation. Not just the words we use, but that air of confidence, our clothes, the equipment we choose to use, our body language. Believe me, the time and effort taken to be more effective in the delivery of your presentation will greatly assist your ultimate negotiation.

To put you on the fast track in preparing for your presentation, we will look at a summary from the bestseller *How to Create and Deliver a Dynamic Presentation*, written by Doug Malouf, published by American Society of Training and Development, and taught to executives throughout the world. Probably its greatest appeal lies in its practical approach to business presentation skills.

The message is quite simple—focus on the key ideas in each presentation and keep the technical words for your next dinner party. (No, on second thought, you don't want to bore the socks off your dinner guests, either. Save the ho-hum technical speeches for your reflection in the mirror.)

Your key ideas are already prepared in the issues that you have identified in the Planning Sheet. These issues provide the basis for everything you do in the Presentation phase.

Let's flip the pages of Doug's book and look at how this process can be used effectively in your next negotiation.

The most natural approach—and the most successful—is to speak in simple, keyword terms.

When the apple fell on Newton's head I'm sure he didn't just rub the sore spot and murmur reflectively: "Yes, well here I am sitting under a twenty-six-year-old tree with red apples about eight centimeters in diameter, one of which has fallen very quickly, impacted on my scalp, and caused an immediate sensation of pain . . ."

It would have been far more in character for him to yell irately:

"Which redneck threw that blasted apple?!!"

This is the way we normally speak. So why don't we speak more naturally at presentations? After all, everyone there is an adult like ourselves. But something seems to happen to people when they have to make a "formal" presentation. They seem to believe that to impress others, to be "correct," they must either speak in gobbledegook or become a technocrat.

Ugh. Forget it.

After almost twenty years in the business of training and public speaking I have found it makes a lot more sense to focus on keywords. This is why Doug's material is so powerful, because he has taken the complex and converted it into the "simplex."

Doug has given me permission to share with you a few practical ideas from his book.

The Apple Tree approach, as Doug calls it, forces you, the negotiator, to prepare only the keywords for the negotiation—and focus only on the "must-knows" for the presentation.

Keywording helps your thinking and cuts out the need for detailed scripting. You actually prepare more quickly, thus saving valuable time.

There are benefits for the people on the other side of the negotiating table, too. Keywording allows them to see the core of your message at a glance. They're far more likely to be impressed by this example of efficiency than by pages of unnecessary information.

So how does this new and innovative approach work? There are five key steps—and the good news is that they are easy to learn and apply:

1. Give your subject material a creative title.
2. Reduce your material to "must-know" statements.
3. Reduce your "must-know's" to keywords.
4. Build mini-speeches around each keyword.
5. Illustrate your mini-speeches, using visuals.

A creative title
It is important to have a theme for your material and to give it a creative or catchy title.

Reduce your material to "must-know" statements
From my experience I have found that to focus on just five "must-know's" is about the upper limit of most audiences' retention capabilities. You know your material, but give it some extra

thought. Brainstorm and list what you feel are the key facts. Now rank them in order of importance from "must-know's" to the "should-know's" to the "nice-to-know's." Select and focus on the top four.

Remember: you have already done this on your Planning Sheet.

Reduce your "must-know's" to keywords

Keywording means condensing the essential message of your information into one easily remembered word or phrase. The keyword you select should be the "key" to the particular subtopic you are discussing.

You may be doubtful about whether you can reduce the negotiation to a few keywords. Isn't the information sometimes too complex?

In a word, no. Keywords are simply the most important points. It helps to clarify your thinking, so work at it. The path to success is the ability to reduce the mass of information into four keywords. It can be done. All it needs is for you to be disciplined.

Build mini-speeches around each keyword

A series of mini-speeches around each keyword is much more interesting than one boring long speech. In your mini-speeches it is important to structure your subtopics in such a way that you

explain it,

reinforce it, and

sell it.

Explain why you have chosen a particular keyword by relating it to the negotiation at hand.

Reinforce the keywords and material using anecdotes, demonstrations, facts, and statistics.

Sell the other side on the concept to at least think about, accept, remember, and act upon your presentation.

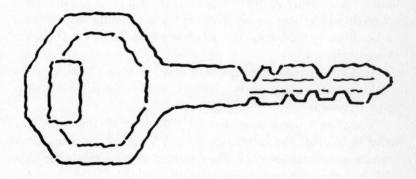

Illustrate your material

Now we all know we can use slides, films, videos, etc., but it is important to create mental pictures through stories, humor, and other stimulants that are relevant to the subject material.

For example, if I were trying to sell you on the "keyword approach" I would first try to think of the main benefit for you in using it—the reduction in the preparation time—as a means of getting you to use it. With this in mind I approached the author, for further advice.

"Doug," I said, plonking the manuscript for this book down on his desk, "I know this Apple Tree approach works, because I've used it successfully so many times myself. But I thought my readers might like to hear a story from the horse's mouth, so to speak."

I pointed at his book, *How to Create and Deliver a Dynamic Presentation.*

"Can you give me an example of how you took a hunk of technical material—some fairly complex stuff—and came up with some keywords?"

"Easy," said Doug immediately. "The example that comes to mind right off is the campaign we did for Apex (an Australian organization) back in 1977. They wanted to raise funds for kids with leukemia. The campaign title was simple, catchy, easy for everyone to remember—it was called 'Help a Kid Make It.'"

I nodded. "OK. So there's the clear, creative title. Then what?"

"They handed me this great two-inch-thick document," he went on. "It wouldn't have looked out of place with a set of encyclopedias! Chock-a-block full of facts, figures, case studies, strategies—the works. From that, they wanted me to come up with the best way of publicizing and presenting a fund-raising project." He shook his head. "Two-aspirin territory!"

"Good," I said. "That's exactly the kind of thing my readers are going to come up against in a negotiation—having to put together a presentation from massive amounts of information, not knowing where to start! So how did you get around the problem?"

"First, I figured out the main need. They wanted to raise funds, right? A million dollars, in fact. Second, they needed a novel way to package the presentation to the public. I knew I had to keep it simple. So—" He snapped his fingers. "—I came up with something short and simple. A number—134567."

What's 134567 got to do with a million bucks, you may ask?

Well, he divided one million by the number of Apex clubs in the country and realized that each club needed to raise $1,345.67 in order to get the million dollars.

Beautiful.

Simple.

Effective.

Many Apex clubs even wrote to Doug and said: "We're not yet sure of the details, but it's for a good cause, so here's our check for $1,345.67."

Combined with the simple title "Help a Kid Make It" and a few other keyword concepts and phrases, the fund-raising project was a tremendous success.

Keep in mind that every time you stand to present your case in a negotiation with the other side, you are costing them, as well as your own side, time and money. Everyone will be grateful if you can prevent time from being dragged out any longer than necessary. Being creative and using the Apple Tree approach will keep your session simple.

Work on your skills of getting to the heart of the subject matter, no matter how technical or complicated it might seem. Leave the details to a supporting handout sheet if necessary. Because if you can't hold the other side's attention, they'll all be daydreaming. They'll be wishing they were outside sitting under an apple tree—or inside perfecting their aerodynamic skills, building paper airplanes. (Maybe, if you're bad enough, they will be building paper airplanes from the pages of all that unnecessary material.)

It's quite simple: give them plain information, not plane-making time.

Having pared your main case down to a few keywords, the other major concern during the Presentation phase of the negotiation is the use of support material in the presentation.

There have been a number of studies over the years concerning the effectiveness of using visual support material during any presentation. The most conclusive studies were completed some years ago by the 3M company and the Wharton School at the University of Pennsylvania.

In the study, 125 candidates studying for their Master's Degrees in Business Administration were asked to persuade a group to introduce a fictional new product. They did this over a series of thirty-six meetings. The pressure was real—the same pressure that you're under when you present your proposal to the other side in the negotiation.

The meetings were structured in such a way as to simulate the evaluations and decision-making processes that would normally take place in a real-life meeting. To examine the impact of using visuals during negotiations, one speaker used visuals presented on the overhead projector, and the other used nothing. All the presenters took turns to try the same experiment, using the whole group as their audience.

The results?

At the end of the eight-week study, comparisons among the speakers showed:

The visuals had an impact on final decisions reached.

The audience perceived the presenters with visuals to be more credible.

The meeting process took less time.

The speakers using visuals were also perceived to be better prepared, more persuasive, and far more professional, and to have created interest in their proposal.

But you probably don't need me to tell you about studies that prove what a difference visuals make. You've been to enough presentations yourself where you're on the receiving end, right? You know whether you'd rather be listening to a speaker who just talks—or one who gives you something other than the cut of his suit to look at.

USING VISUALS

Here are some useful tips on using visuals during the negotiation Presentation phase.

Remember this principle: Less Is Best.

Use only the keywords and the "must-know's" as the basis for your visuals. Nigel King, an expert on the preparation of visuals at the 3M company, advocates four simple rules:

1. No more than six lines per visual
2. No more than six words per line
3. Use graphics
4. Add impact with color

This forces you to keep the words to an absolute minimum. The same applies to the number of visuals being used. Keep them to a minimum. People will get bored if you're slapping up one overhead after another—anything overdone will lose its impact.

On the other hand, a few carefully selected, well-prepared visuals are memorable and assist the other side in understanding your proposal.

Doug Malouf agrees wholeheartedly, saying: "I'm convinced that one of the reasons the Apex campaign was so successful was the use of visuals to sell the presentation."

If it's possible to use color, do so. It will help stimulate the other side in the decision-making process. The 3M company can show you how you can turn a full-color photographic or 35mm slide into a full-color visual to help in the negotiation.

A number of major negotiations have been won from competing proposals in the Presentation phase because of being perceived as better organized and more professional—largely due to their use of carefully chosen visuals.

Of course, I'm bound to have offended a few great orators out there who think using visuals is a waste of time. However, the studies are conclusive:

Visuals are more persuasive and are time efficient.

I have to say at this stage that I can project plenty of personality and enthusiasm when I want to. I know I can charm the other side through selective use of language in my presentation— but this is not enough to succeed in a presentation. Visual messages are powerful.

If you don't believe me, there are plenty of others who feel the same way—and have backed it up with research.

To give one example:

Recent studies from Columbia University show that our message is normally interpreted by the receiver in the following percentages:

1.5% Touch

1.5% Taste

6.0% Smell

11.0% Hearing

80.0% Visual

The message is clear. Use visuals, make them interesting, and you will be more successful and credible in your next negotiation.

CHARTS AND GRAPHS

Too often charts and graphs in a presentation give the other side another reason to daydream or go to sleep. Use them with caution. If you have to use charts and graphs, the following ideas will serve as a simple guideline in their application.

The time to use charts, graphs, and tables is when you are presenting to the other side information and data involving some form of comparison or trend. It might be in the form of comparing an old system to your proposed system.

Remember K.I.S.S.—Keep It Super Simple.

How do you know what kind of charts to use?

When you want to show trends, use a Line Chart. They are useful to illustrate trends or make comparative analyses, especially when your proposal is the best line.

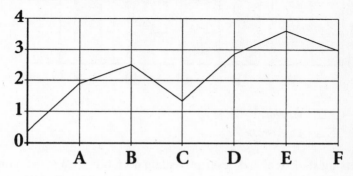

If you are trying to depict ratios, proportions, parts relative to a whole, use a Pie Chart. This is useful when showing how the divided elements share a total of the whole picture.

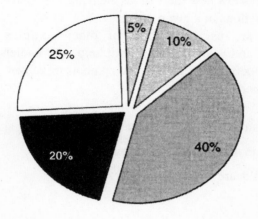

Contrast can be displayed by the use of Bar Charts. Interesting results can be achieved when different symbols are used creatively as the bars. Examples could be documents, automobiles, airplanes, anything that can depict your message visually.

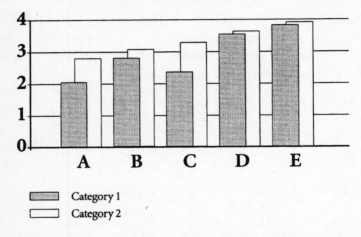

Using statistical and descriptive data normally means everyone keeps pinching themselves to keep awake. Use Tables and Columns to present information of similar values, usually numerical data related to a series of measurements.

If you are showing steps in a flow diagram, use Block Diagrams to show how the various elements are used to represent specific functions in a given operation.

If you are using symbols or other complex material, Schematics and Scale Drawings will help your audience to visualize the importance of the various symbols or values.

Remember:

If you can make your message visual, do it.

If you can add impact by using color, do it.

The results are well worth it.

PRESENTATION TECHNIQUES

When you finally come to present your proposal, here are some simple ideas that will add impact to the use of the overhead projector and the visuals you use in the presentation:

1. Before you turn the overhead projector on, place the visual in position, making sure it's right side up, with the heading exposed. If it's a very important negotiation, don't rely on equipment provided by the other side. Bring your own overhead projector. The same advice applies if you are using a computer projection panel; make sure it works before the presentation starts.

2. Use what is known as the "revelation technique." That is, you place a piece of paper over the visual and reveal only the part of the information that you want the other side to see when you turn the projector on. Once you have explained each point, you can then move the paper down to the next point and continue until the whole visual has been revealed.

3. If you want to build a reasonably detailed picture for the other side, use the overlay technique. This allows you to start with a base visual and then add more visuals on the top to build the picture or complexity of detail you want.

4. Use a pointer on the projector, if required. Never turn and point to the screen. Too often nervous presenters spend all their time talking to the screen and not the other party.

What about using 35mm slides in the Presentation phase? There is no doubt that they can be very useful, but the drawback is that you need to have the lights out. If it has been a long day, those on the other side could use the opportunity to catch a surreptitious forty winks.

You just don't have the immediate flexibility with 35mm that you have with an overhead projector and visuals. Slide presentations can be great, but remember, it takes time to prepare them.

Finally, make sure you practice with the equipment.

Time

The effectiveness of your presentation—not to mention the eventual success or failure of your negotiation—could hinge on the time of day of the presentation. From my own experience, and that of many other presenters and negotiators, I urge you to schedule the presentation either in the morning or close to lunch.

Most of us are at our freshest in the morning. Our critical thinking is at its peak. From a practical negotiating point, if a break is necessary and you have started in the morning, you can reconvene in the afternoon.

If the other side requests a late afternoon or early evening session, you need to be assertive and ask why. Then you need to decide if the answer is valid. If it isn't, then arrange the meeting time to suit you.

It is important to emphasize again at this point the feeling that both sides have a level playing ground. The other party needs you as much as you need them.

Timing is very much like seating. If you feel uncomfortable— do something about it before the meeting starts!

Body language

There is a very important factor in any presentation that often gets scant attention from negotiators—the issue of body language. The last thing you need is for your nervousness to cause a ripple effect that has the other side becoming nervous during the presentation.

This is important not only from your viewpoint, but also from that of the other side.

Deliver the message in a positive mode. Have all the information at your fingertips; smile and speak slowly. Nervousness can make you speed up your presentation, or you may run out of

breath. Your voice may squeak, your sentences could lose punch at the end.

If you start to panic, stop and have a drink of water. Deliberately slow the pace. You can't afford to send out negative vibes with your body language. There are many great books and videos available on this subject; take the time to work your way through them.

THE BIG DAY

The big day has arrived.

You have gone to the boardroom of Real Big Spenders to present your proposal for a consulting contract for the next twelve months. You have presented the ideas, and the mood is positive.

Then things start to go wrong.

Halfway through the second point (concerning payment), the other side becomes heated. Voices quiver, mouths become grim. Their body language shows that you have hit a raw nerve.

What do you do?

1. Remember that in any negotiation, disagreements will occur from the moment you say "let's negotiate" to the final agreement. If you can, have the matter put to one side until you have finished the whole of your presentation—otherwise each point will become a minefield. If the other side becomes emotional about the issue, make sure you deal with the emotion, not the issue. Don't give any concessions just for the sake of keeping the meeting going. Some people will use this as a tactic to wear you down during the presentation, so it's important that you don't lose sight of where you're up to in the whole negotiation. Remember, your mission at this stage is to complete your presentation, not to bargain over each point made.

2. Make a note of any concern and move on to the next part of the presentation. This indicates that you are listening, but more important, ensures that you still have control over the presentation.

3. Don't give too much information away when answering questions, because the other side will still try to use this part of the presentation as a means of establishing your position in the negotiation.

4. Once you have handled the various questions, move on and complete the presentation.

The key is to know that the Presentation phase is setting the groundwork for the Bargaining phase. Too much emotion and too little substance can muddy the waters for the Bargaining phase.

Do your preparation, and the Presentation phase is easy.

If you don't prepare, disaster will dog your every step. Let's look at a recent example where all sides came into the Presentation phase for the purpose of saber-rattling, without trying to establish an environment for agreement.

The Middle East peace talks in the early 1990s at Madrid in Spain are a classic example of where disaster struck in the Presentation phase.

The concerns were emotive and not based on the true issues to be negotiated. Both Israel and its Arab counterparts used the Presentation phase of their peace negotiations to throw insults and dredge up old grievances instead of concentrating on issues.

All this really achieved was for both sides to become involved in a battle of egos. If you are looking at achieving mutually satisfying agreements, naturally this can't work.

Remember:

The purpose of the Presentation phase is to set the foundations for reaching agreement, not to compare muscle.

Always stick to the phase that you're in.

Keep in mind that the other side just might be on to you, and could be using this as a clever tactic to try to get you caught up in emotive issues.

Finally, if this is a deliberate negotiation you are entering into, know that you are trying to improve your relationship with the other side, not score points. You should be using this phase as a means of increasing the level of trust between you and the other organization.

The Presentation phase is a chance to show quite clearly why they should be doing business with you and not against you!

SUMMARY

1. Think in terms of three easy steps:

   Adopt the role of a good defense lawyer

   Prepare the other side's case

   Present the reason for your case being better

2. Map out the negotiation Planning Sheet, and, in putting it all together, use all the strategies we have talked about in earlier chapters:

   Move along the quick/deliberate continuum

   Allow for Realistic, Acceptable, and Worst Possible outcomes

   Identify four key issues to work with

   By using four issues and three different outcomes you give yourself a great many options; eighty-one, to be precise.

3. Make the presentation to the other side.

Chapter 6

The Bargaining Phase

"Utterly worthless!" says the buyer as he haggles over the price. But afterward he brags about the bargain.

— *After* Proverbs 20:14

Once you've been in on a few negotiations, you'll note that "hard-nosed" negotiators often seem to come out in front. They may not end up with too many friends at the end of the day, but still, you half admire the way they can take things right down to the wire and get what they want.

That's the sign of a good negotiator, isn't it?

Well, no—not necessarily. They may win a negotiation, but their opponents rarely come back for repeat business. The negotiators on the other side who are looking for a cooperative approach resulting in mutual gains are not greatly impressed with this win-at-all-costs approach.

Let me share with you a story about a tough negotiator—we'll call him Hardy Nayles.

Hardy believed that the best way to survive in the world was to make sure he always negotiated the best deal for himself at the expense of the other side. He was so good at it that half the time the other side didn't even realize they were being ripped off. I guess you'd say that most of the time he was successful in his negotiations. Not well-liked, true, but successful.

One day our intrepid negotiator decided he needed a break. A holiday seemed like a good idea—and he had heard about just the place: a magic lake in the middle of a fantasyland called the Place of Mirrors.

"You must go," urged previous vacation goers. "Get right away from the real world. This place is amazing. All you have to do is take one drink from those magic waters and you'll find yourself making brilliant decisions without having to think about it!"

Hardy Nayles packed his bags. A place where being a success without even having to work at it sounded like just the spot for a hard-nosed negotiator to relax. Pushing people to the brink all the time to get the best deal was a lot of hard work.

Hardy found it more difficult than he expected to adjust to the Place of Mirrors. The inhabitants really were an appallingly inefficient lot—why, when he tried to hire a boat, there wasn't even anyone minding the shop. A toothless old man, basking in the sun, informed him that there was a big horse race in some southern land, and everyone had taken the afternoon off.

Annoyed, Hardy decided simply to take the boat he wanted. It wasn't as though anyone seemed to care—this was obviously a land with no sense of responsibility. He was getting worried that his negotiating skills would become rusty, with no one to beat down to a better price.

Even the fish didn't seem to be fulfilling their part of the bargain. If this was such a great holiday spot, why weren't they biting? After a few hours he was beginning to wonder if all the fish had gone to the same horse race, when at last there was a tug on the line.

The fish put up a good fight and adrenalin rushed through Hardy's veins. At last, he triumphantly hauled the fish over the side. Closer examination showed it to be a very strange fish indeed. Brilliant blue, its scales flashed in the sunlight as it thrashed about in the bottom of the boat. Startled, Hardy realized the fish was looking at him with a distinctly intelligent glint in its eye.

Then it spoke.

"Please throw me back in the lake," begged the fish. "If you do, I'll grant you three wishes."

Three wishes? Hardy Nayles smiled. Three wishes would make a big difference to his life, but imagine what his future would be like if he could get this weird fish up to **five**? He didn't have a reputation as Hard-As-Nails Hardy for nothing.

"Make it five," he suggested, leaning back casually and watching the desperate fish. "And we've got a deal."

"I can only grant three," gasped the fish pleadingly.

"Four and a half," said Nayles, indifferently inspecting his fingernails.

"Three," said the fish, barely breathing.

The tough negotiator folded his arms and pretended to consider the offer.

"Okay," he said. "We'll compromise on four wishes."

This time, the fish did not reply. It lay dead on the bottom of the boat.

I grant you, the message contained in this story is not subtle! It's not meant to be. On the contrary, the message from this story is clear—if you have got to the Bargaining phase of a deliberate negotiation and then approach the other side like good ol' Hardy Nayles—you've blown it. An agreement will be difficult, if not impossible, to reach.

In our workshops we often use structured activities to show how easy it is to be a Hardy Nayles—that is, being a winner by beating the other side. A lot of participants who negotiate this way feel that their early successes show the world that they are good negotiators.

However, these people don't do too well in the next exercise—because no one in the group trusts them enough to do business with them! What happens in training also happens in real-life situations. If the word gets around that you're a Hard-As-Nails type, you can end up doing your company a disservice simply by undertaking their negotiations.

You must remember that in this phase of the negotiation you should be adopting the role of **Judge**.

Your role here, like a judge in court, is to listen to both sides of the story before responding. You also need to have finely honed questioning skills—first, to bring out the facts, and second, to become aware of the different tactics each side will use to win their case.

Let's suppose for a moment that the negotiator on the other side wants to play tough. They're not interested in working in a cooperative manner. What do you do? To find the answer, we'll look at common tactics used by competitive negotiators in an attempt to get a better deal. Then we will examine the issue of our **perception** of how powerful the other side appears. Too often we believe that they are more powerful than ourselves. This is dangerous.

Remember again, if they have come this far, they need you as much as you need them.

In earlier chapters we looked at how the needs and motivation we have directly affects how we behave toward the other side during the Bargaining phase.

Our motivation dictates our whole approach.

You will know from experience that the more you want a deal to happen, the harder it is for you to remain neutral in the Bargaining phase. The more emotionally involved you are in a negotiation, the more you tend to concede and give away in the Bargaining phase.

So it's vital to be aware of how emotionally involved you are in the next negotiation. This knowledge gives you a better chance of remaining objective. (In chapter 8, we'll take this concept one step further by examining the dynamics of team negotiations.)

The types of behavior and moral values that people bring to the bargaining table have been discussed for centuries. Did you know that you'll even find recommendations on behavior in business negotiations in the Bible?

The advice in the Book of Proverbs is quite clear:

Be fair in your business dealings. If you are to bargain, don't adopt an adversarial role in an attempt to get a better price.

It's obvious that even in the days before Christ, people would adopt a strong position on price and then brag about their gains to their friends.

There are plenty of ways to evaluate the other side's responses during the Bargaining phase. Probably the most useful is to analyze the use of tactics, so that's what we'll do. Since the perception of power versus the reality of power can influence the outcome of a negotiation so dramatically, we'll take a look at that too, and then finish off with a quick run-through of effective questioning techniques.

TACTICS

At seminar after seminar, participants ask the same question:

"When is it the right time to use tactics in a negotiation?"

The answer to that is: if you are serious about negotiating (especially when using the cooperative style), there is only **one** tactic that you should use—and use wisely.

The Walk-Away tactic

Your ability to be able to get up and walk away from the table without closing a deal will set you apart from the rest.

You may walk away with an idea of returning to the bargaining table at a later time, or you may totally disengage. **Good negotiators know when to call it a day.**

The Walk-Away tactic can be used at any time during a negotiation: whether it's while discussing the agenda, the location for the negotiation, or how the seats are to be arranged.

The key is to use it as **part of your planning**.

Don't jump to its use because you have been upset by the other side. Skillfully applied, the Walk-Away becomes a great asset in all your negotiations.

The other side, if not negotiating ethically, will use any dirty trick available to them. We will look at the most popular tactics that will be used against you—

The twelve Hollywood Classics!

There are no doubt many more, but experience and research show these to be the most common.

Once in a while you will be tempted to stoop to the level of using tactics such as these to achieve success. **Don't be tempted**. If you are serious about negotiating, you will not need any tricks.

You'll probably see these tactics in the classic movies of bygone days, but rest assured—they're rarely used in reality by top-line negotiators. However, it is essential that you are prepared for them. Be ready for these tactics to be used on you when you **first meet** the other side, **during** the negotiation, or when you are **about to sign** the deal. Note, too, that they seem to be regularly used regardless of where you are negotiating in the world.

The list is not in any order of priority, and you might even know the tactics mentioned by another name—but the outcome is just the same.

THE HOLLYWOOD CLASSICS

Emotional outburst

This is a tactic that is used when the other side wants to exercise their power and shorten the time of the negotiation. It is usually in the form of an outburst of anger or emotional hype. Stand back and coolly assess the outburst, and you'll find that it is very seldom directed toward the issues being negotiated. It is always directed toward you, so that you'll be unsettled for the rest of the negotiation.

Once you're aware of this, it loses most of its power over you. The most effective way to respond, although it will test your powers of self-control, is by not responding in kind. An angry

response from you will only prolong this tactic. Remember, too, that we say things in anger that can't be retrieved at a later time.

One of the other options to use to overcome this tactic is to suggest a break and return to the negotiation when everyone has calmed down.

If the other side persists, it's okay to let them know that you are feeling frustrated. Don't be tempted to blame the other side for this. Simply say something like: "I am feeling frustrated!" This will allow you to express how you feel without angering the other side. They will quickly get the message.

Argue a special case

This tends to be frequently used in negotiations between labor and management over pay and conditions. Most of the time it is used without any reference to previous awards or decisions. It is very important, when this is used early in a negotiation, to **identify** the special case—without accusing the other side of lying or even worse.

One of the most effective ways of handling this tactic is by not responding until you've had time to consider the demands. Request a break, and get back to them with hard data—get the facts.

Pretend ignorance

This is one of the classics. It's well used by seasoned negotiators. It is used to draw you out with the aim of extracting more information from you in the early stages. You are up against a smooth operator when this is used against you.

Did you ever see the television series *Columbo*? The scruffy detective hero used the pretense of innocence to great effect! Like Columbo, its modern users find it a wonderfully sneaky way of extracting extra information. Remember, he would always ask one last question!

One of the most effective ways of handling this approach is by answering only the question asked and volunteering nothing further—especially information about your case. The key here is to answer the question, then shut up.

Environment

This is a favored tactic with global negotiations. The other side can set up the environment any way they choose, so that they can have a psychological advantage by being on their own turf. They have access to all their resources and can put you anywhere they wish.

If you do go to the other side's company headquarters and find yourself left alone in a small room for twenty minutes, all your senses should be on red alert. They are preparing you as a sacrifice.

You can handle this tactic by being firm but fair and requesting neutral ground. If they won't play ball, then make sure you're involved at least in deciding where you're seated—and also the actual seating arrangements for the whole meeting.

"You go first"

Deciding the relative merits of going first in a negotiation is a bit like the dilemma faced by the coach of a football team. If you win the toss at the beginning of a game, do you elect to kick off or receive? Different people will give you different advice.

Each negotiation is different. Sometimes I prefer to go first. At other times I am quite happy to listen. But you're probably thinking that this sit-on-the-fence type of advice is not much use.

So I'll suggest a rule of thumb:

If you are the seller, opt to go first—with, of course, an outstanding presentation. I recommend this because you know their "greatest pain" and can (we hope) fix it through your offer of the proposed solution.

If you are the buyer, it is always wise to let the seller go first because you will then know what the full package is going to cost you. If you're still in doubt, give careful thought to the nature of the buyer/seller relationship. You'll find it a useful guide.

Ultimatum

This tactic is used quite often when the other side is trying to bully you into a quick decision. It's a common tactic when people are trying to get you to buy a business or new product. You're likely to hear something along the lines of: "It's a golden opportunity to make a lot of easy money—you can't afford to miss the chance!"

First, there's no such thing as an easy way to make money. Second, those types of opportunities are like buses: if you miss one, another will come along before too long.

How do you handle the ultimatum?

One of the most effective ways is to review before making a decision. The pressure to say yes will be overwhelming, but be strong.

(Remember the old saying, "Decide in haste, repent at leisure.")

Time

This is another of the classic tactics in both global and domestic negotiations. If you have allowed x number of days to set the deal and find yourself twiddling your thumbs while nothing is being discussed, you can bet that all the meaty parts will be negotiated on the way back to the airport.

Time is also used as a tactic for drawing out the day's proceedings so that an eight-hour day becomes a twelve-hour day. The pressure of time is used to make you decide when you are very tired.

To combat this one, negotiate the time agenda with the other side right at the start of the proceedings, then stick to it.

The nibble

This is a clever tactic that is normally used toward the end of the negotiation. It is used to "nibble" a little more from the seller to get a better deal. This one is a classic with organizations that have purchased office equipment or large quantities of a product.

The nibble normally appears in the guise of an offhand remark like: "By the way, we will get ninety-day terms, or a 10 percent discount, won't we. . . ?"

This is a particularly vulnerable time for the seller, and, unfortunately, most succumb to the pressure. As a seller you are vulnerable because you fear that if you don't agree you may lose the deal. It is a tactic that works only too well on too many occasions.

If you do give in, ask for a concession in return. For instance, if it's a big deal, ask for C.O.D. instead of terms.

Do try to remain firm, though: it is better to remain firm and even start the negotiation over again, if need be. Remember, the key is to reduce any dollar or percentage figure by small and steady increments. Too quick and it will appear that your initial offer was overly inflated.

Higher authority

This tactic works by getting all the information from you and then putting the pressure on you by stalling for time. You won't usually find this tactic being used up front when you are setting the agenda, but rather when it comes to decision-making time.

This is quite a clever tactic, because the other side will try to get you to accept a lesser offer by indicating that something better would "have to be approved by a higher authority in the organization." Many a poor deal has been put together by using this tactic.

You'll be able to outmaneuver any negotiator seeking to use this ploy by exploring the other side's authority level when you are setting the agenda.

Silence

Silence is a tactic used by seasoned and well-experienced negotiators. If you find that you are doing more than 50 percent of the talking, watch out—the other person is using your loose lips to find out how far they can push you.

If you ask a question and fail to get an answer from the other side, don't jump in and answer for them. You will end up giving away the shop and your shirt with your nervous expansiveness.

Filling the silence by answering your own questions will let the other side know very quickly that you are new to the field of negotiating.

You can turn this tactic back on them by using **active listening** (we'll talk more about this in a moment). Ask a question, then shut up. If the question is not answered by the other side, then you know they are using the "silent treatment" as a tactic.

That's our contract

This one is especially important when you are dealing with professional people and the government. The fact that a piece of paper has the word "agreement" or "contract" written on the top of it means very little.

This tactic is used to intimidate you by suggesting that the contract, because of its official-looking nature, is unable to be altered. You'll inevitably find, upon reading this type of document, that it is weighted heavily against you.

You can handle this tactic by having the document altered and then handing it back to the other side. This will soon show if they are really interested.

Good guy/bad guy

You know this tactic very well—it's in plenty of the Hollywood detective movies. The other side will hit you with a pair of negotiators. One of them will be the "bad guy"—the tough, mean one who really socks it to you. The other one will seem to be "helping" you—this one's the "good guy" (even if he's not wearing a white hat).

This tactic is still used on a regular basis in nearly all negotiations. Here's the scenario:

The good guy from the other side will always make a low offer that sounds okay, but which will promptly be thrown out by the bad guy.

The good guy will then offer it again: "Look, grab it while you can before Mary comes back . . ." This is used to make you decide quickly. The good guy will always act as if he or she is acting in your best interests. As soon as someone says, "Trust me!" in a negotiation, you've got problems.

One of the most effective ways for handling this tactic is to call the good guy/bad guy together and let them know that you know what they are doing.

If you feel that any one or a combination of the Hollywood Classics are being used on you during the negotiation, **don't** respond emotionally. Address the tactic and get on with the negotiation. Nor should you feel so intimidated by the use of their tactics that you feel you can't challenge them—"they are more powerful than I am." If you feel that you are the weaker one, it's time to challenge your perception of power.

CREATIVITY!

Some time ago a story appeared in one of the local papers that I believe sums up quite nicely how perception in the Bargaining phase can affect the outcomes.

A five-year-old boy went to the barbershop to get his first grown-up haircut.

"Hello," said the barber. "How would you like it?"

"Just like my dad's," said the little boy. "**With a hole on top!**"

The little boy was using all his experience by responding in the way that he did. He had never experienced a haircut before, so he thought perceptively before he responded. (I guess it would have been a creative barber, too, that could have cut his hair with a hole in the top!)

There are two major blocks to being a successful negotiator. One is failure in being creative, both during the negotiation and when preparing for it. The ability to think creatively will greatly enhance your success. (This will be dealt with in detail in chapter 9.)

The other block is inability to handle the use of **power** by the other side during a negotiation. Having enough self-control to refrain from responding in the attack mode during a negotiation will also increase the chances of both sides being successful.

Now, let's have a look at the **perception** of power—that is, how powerful you perceive the other side to be, regardless of whether or not this happens to be true.

PERCEPTION OF POWER

✔ If you go into a negotiation convinced that the other organization—or individual—is superior to you, you're likely not only to lose the negotiation, but to come out of it somewhat singed.

The key to survival lies in a certain attitude that we adopt even before we start preparing for the negotiation—the attitude we have toward the concept of power in any negotiation. To understand the use of "power" in a negotiation, you first need to understand the difference between perception and reality.

The experience of the Japanese army in World War II will give you some insight into how this works.

During the Second World War when the Japanese army was sweeping through most of Southeast Asia, they came to Singapore as their next target. They discovered that something like 50,000 troops were guarding Singapore. The enemy were not only far stronger in numbers; they had also had time to prepare their defenses. In stark contrast, the Japanese troops attacking Singapore numbered about 20,000. Incredibly, the British decided to surrender to the Japanese.

How did this come about?

The Japanese, through stories and radio propaganda, created the impression that they couldn't be stopped. It was the most astounding capitulation in the history of the British empire.

The **reality** was that the British had greater numbers and could have defended Singapore. However, their **perception** was that the Japanese force was far greater than it actually was! The outcome of the war might have been totally different if a number of decisions hadn't been made at that time. What made

the leaders of the time decide in the way that they did? It was their **perception** of the situation, not the **reality**.

If there is anything that will destroy your negotiation, even before you start, it will be your belief that the other side is far stronger, wiser, bigger, having better products, or whatever.

The same misconception led to Goliath's downfall in the Biblical story of David and Goliath.

As you can recall, Goliath was a giant of a man in the Philistine army and wanted to destroy the Israelites. Goliath was in the habit of coming down daily to intimidate the Israelites, hurling insults and demanding that a champion come forward and fight him. David, a shepherd boy, accepted the challenge. People looked at the slight child and scoffed. Saul, the King of the Israelites, tried to convince David that he would be committing suicide. Loosely translated, Saul told him: "You can't go against this Philistine to fight him! You're only a boy, and he's been a warrior all his life."

Saul's **perception** was that David would be slaughtered. David's approach to **reality** was with a slingshot and five smooth stones. The rest is history. The story contains a great lesson for all negotiators.

Two things come out of the story of David destroying Goliath:

1. David acted bravely: **even though he didn't have power over Goliath, he acted as if he did.** His conditioning did not tell him that he wouldn't be successful. If he believed that there was a difference, he would have been beaten.

2. Goliath acted as if the battle was already won: **he had power, but then acted as if he didn't**. He viewed David as a joke, took off his helmet, and was destroyed. His conditioning said: "Ha! I am mightier—I will crush him."

The reality was that he couldn't do so.

Do you think Goliath would have been beaten if he had viewed David as equal? It would have been most unlikely.

Think about the last negotiation in which you were involved where your perception of the other side's power greatly exceeded the reality.

What was the outcome of the negotiation?

Did you fail because your perception of the other side's power was greater than it actually was? If so, how can we minimize the risk of perception overruling reality?

The answer is simple:

Enter into every negotiation with the feeling that both sides are equal. Then you will be on an equal footing. If you can't do that, go to the negotiation with a sling and five stones—and imagine that you are David facing your own Goliath!

Want a test of how habits can form our perceptions?

Do this:

Next time you go to a busy office building or hotel, stand back and watch how often people will push the elevator button.

It doesn't make the elevator come any quicker, but the perception is that it will!

USE THE THREE Q'S

When in doubt during the Bargaining phase of the negotiation, use the three Q's: Questions, Questions, Questions!

You are looking at ways of influencing and persuading the other side that your options are viable enough for an agreement to be reached. At this point in the negotiation, too many negotiators try to open up the other side by making statements and hoping that they will respond.

This normally does not work. All it does is offer the other side the opportunity to receive more information from us, or react emotionally to our comments.

There are three reasons why you should use questions instead of statements in the Bargaining phase of the negotiation:

1. Questions allow the other side to tell you about their needs and wants for the outcome of the negotiation. You'll be able to find out in far greater detail what they want to achieve as a result of the negotiation.

2. Once the other side begins to open up and share their feelings and opinions, they are starting to make an investment in the outcome. It moves from being a discussion to a way of reaching agreement.

3. We stand a far better chance of persuading someone by the skillful use of questions, than by making emotive statements.

This is the phase of the negotiation where concessions are offered, traded, and agreed to. Your use of questions will make sure that process works successfully for you. The use of questions instead of statements actively involves the other side. Once that happens, agreement is not too far away.

However, adept questioning is a skill. Don't think any old questions will do the trick. Some questions you ask will encourage the other side to open up to you—others will cause them to stop talking. It's essential that you know the right kind of question to ask at the right time.

What we'll be looking at here are the three most commonly used questions in negotiations:

1. Open
2. Closed
3. Reflective

Open questions
Open-type questions are very effective in getting the other side to open up in the negotiation. They are useful in seeking clarification,

generally gaining more information, and encouraging a detailed response.

You can identify this type of question by the first word— open-style questions normally begin with *How, What, When, Where, Who*, and *Why*.

We'll use our ongoing example of the "Sale Of House By Owner" advertisement. Here are some examples of open-type questions:

"How do you feel about the options we have discussed so far?"

"What do you think about the finance details?"

"When do you plan to approach your banker?"

"Where are you planning to have the final meeting?"

"Who else has made you an offer as good as ours?"

"Why do you say that my offer is laughable?"

Remember, the point of open-type questions is to gain information from the other side. You want their opinions, feelings, and reactions to your ideas so far. Get them talking through questions.

Closed questions

Closed questions will net you a straightforward yes or no type of response from the other side. You'll want to use these questions when you are not looking for information, data, or a clue about their feelings. They are designed to get a quick response. They are effective when checking details in the early stages of the negotiation. Here are some examples:

"Have you read my proposal?"

"Do you intend settling today?"

Closed-type questions are used when you need only a little information and want to move the process along.

Reflective questions

The reflective type of question is, in effect, like holding up a mirror to the other side. It is designed to allow you to respond to their answer with another question.

Its usefulness is that you repeat their answer in your own words to confirm or clarify your understanding of their answer.

"You feel that the offer is too low?"

"The possession date is too soon. Is that what you are saying?"

"So you believe that the offer is still too low. How far apart are we?"

Reflective-type questions are useful for maintaining the negotiation when you don't want to upset the other side.

Reflective listening skills are powerful—they are commonly used by therapists to encourage their patients to talk; reflective listening skills are taught to nurses, social workers, and recruits in police academies. They are part of parent effectiveness courses and teacher effectiveness courses. Learn to use these skills, and you will be in a far better position in any negotiation.

I must sound one warning note: there are many books available that will try to tell you the exact words to use during the Bargaining phase of the negotiation. Don't be tempted to buy them.

Be yourself in the Bargaining phase. Use questions that suit your own style and personality, and you will be successful in reaching many agreements. Learn the skills, but don't learn the rote questions. This is real life, not a school quiz.

The Bargaining phase is the danger zone, where we risk losing our cool because the other side turns up the heat and we fall into the trap of responding in anger. You can improve the odds for your team dramatically by using the advice given in this chapter.

If you have prepared and if you have worked out your Planning Sheet, the Bargaining phase will only enhance your ability to turn no into yes.

SUMMARY

1. Use creativity.
2. Be aware of the perception of power versus the reality of power.
3. Be prepared for unethical methods (The Hollywood Classics). But don't use them yourself.
4. The only "tactic" you ever need: the Walk-Away.
5. Why you should use questions instead of statements in the Bargaining phase of the negotiation.

Chapter 7

The Agreement Phase

You've got to know when to hold 'em,
know when to fold 'em,
know when to walk away,
and know when to run!

—Kenny Rogers, "The Gambler"

Well, it's been a challenging voyage, but we're almost ready to furl the sails and relax. You should be proud of yourself. You have negotiated the stormy waters of the Bargaining phase; kept in mind the reality of where the power lies; kept a weather eye out for the Hollywood Classics, and used skillful, open-ended questions to involve the other side. Having argued your case with dexterity and skill, you have safely arrived at the Agreement phase. This is, without a doubt, one of the most important parts of the Negotiation Model. Now you need to make critical decisions. Detailed agreements must be made.

The most critical considerations in this phase are

who is going to make the final decision,

where the actual agreement is to take place, and

the timing of the agreement.

Since this phase is where the specific details of the negotiation will be agreed to, it is essential at all times to use active listening skills to reach decisions, but particularly when handling any objections. The last thing you want is to get this far and then sabotage all the work you've put in because of inattention.

You need to be on your guard against not only the timing and location of the meeting but also the level of risk-taking adopted.

Given the myriad details you have to keep in mind in this phase, you can understand why the role you will now find most effective is that of Accountant. Each detail must be checked with utmost care. Any inconsistencies in the draft agreement must be discovered before you give the final nod. It's no good saying, "Oops, there's something out of place here" after the deal is done.

The physical surroundings in the Agreement phase can have a subtle (or not-so-subtle!) influence on the outcome of the negotiation. Don't underestimate the importance of where the negotiation should be finalized.

PLACE

Where is the most effective place to reach the final agreement?

Should it be their place, your place, or neutral ground? That question can only be answered by your taking into consideration all the facts available at the time. For example, if the style is going to be a quick, competitive negotiation, then most of the negotiations will automatically take place on their turf. If you find that all your negotiations are taking place on their turf, regardless of the type of negotiation, then I recommend that you start looking at the way you classify your negotiations.

You're probably not thinking clearly about what you want out of each negotiation. Will there be an ongoing relationship? Is their goodwill important to you? And so on. Another possibility is that you're treating each negotiation as a battle of wills.

If the negotiation is one where you are adopting the cooperative style in order to build positive business relationships, it's quite okay to agree to negotiations on their turf, so long as you feel there's no hidden agenda.

For instance:

The other side has gone to a lot of trouble in setting up a meeting with other decision makers. They request you meet and present your facts on their ground. There's nothing wrong with that, as long as you feel comfortable with their reasoning.

If for some intuitive reason you do feel uncomfortable, then request neutral ground. To keep the meeting positive you'll have to outline valid, noncombative reasons for wanting neutral territory. Be tactful, and I'm sure that you will not have any problems with the decision.

"What about using tape recorders?" is another question that crops up regularly.

Hmmm. I'd tread carefully here. Every time I have seen recorders used, a certain level of distrust creeps into the meeting.

Creative solutions can be stifled because of the fear that every word is being recorded for posterity. If in doubt, don't use one.

Let's look at some specific questions about the place chosen for your agreement:

Formal or informal setting?

First, decide on one of the three locations (their place, your place, or neutral ground). Then you need to decide whether it will be a formal or informal setting.

The number of participants on both sides of the negotiation will guide your decision. If it is a team negotiation, make sure you know the numbers involved. If it's a one-on-one negotiation, you could opt for either a formal meeting room or a quiet table at a local restaurant.

Formality and informality are conveyed by more than business suits and polished meeting tables, or subdued lighting in a pleasant restaurant.

You need to be very much aware of the "messages" conveyed to the other side by a number of elements: the size of the room, provision (or lack of) whiteboards, seating arrangements, and so on. Here are some of the unspoken messages conveyed by the setting you choose:

Room size

- Large room, small team(s). Message: be on your guard. This is a formal negotiation; not much room to move on either side.

- Small room, small team(s). Message: we want to work toward a solution, not create more tension.

- Medium-sized room. Message: okay, we're happy to involve you in the process.

Whiteboards/newsprint pads/overhead projector

- Message: we're ready to look at options. Let's work together.

Seating arrangements

Having made the decision about where the presentation will take place, you now need to cast that cool Accountant's eye over the seating arrangements.

It's probably no secret to you that seating can be used as part of a process of intimidation. I've proved this to group after group in training sessions by this simple experiment: I allow one team of negotiators to sit on comfortable seats, leaning on the desk, while the other side sits on lower, uncomfortable seats away from the desk.

Deliberately confrontationist?

Yes.

Result?

Exactly what you would expect. The team on the lower, at-a-distance seats felt intimidated. They were at a disadvantage from the start.

If you want meaningful discussions (as I assume most sensible negotiators do) then a round table is very convenient. You can maintain eye contact, and it encourages open discussion when you finally get to the Agreement phase.

What if you're working with a large team negotiation? Well, you can still use a round table, but it might mean that observers and other people have to sit away from the main work area.

Whatever the physical limitations of the area, try at all times to arrange the seating so that you have the best chance for genuine communication.

Now for the dirty tricks department. (Oh, yes, again! The negotiating world's full of them.) You've already seen, in other stages of the negotiation, that some people will use whatever leverage they can to come out on top. Seating is an obvious opportunity to play the power game. When you walk into a room, assess the layout quickly and ask yourself if you feel comfortable with it. If not, don't go ahead with the negotiation until it's changed. Otherwise you'll find that you are worrying more about your own concerns and psychological needs than the negotiation.

Although there are no definite rules of "right" or "wrong" when it comes to seating arrangements, you'll quickly learn that certain arrangements go hand in hand with positive or negative settings. So here are a couple of timely hints about what you may encounter and what you can do to fix it.

- Your presentation is one on one and the other side is seated behind a desk in a bigger and better chair. Message: this creates an aura of power—for them. You might be approaching the negotiation from a cooperative point of view, but the message conveyed by the seating is "I'm in charge. I'll be making the decisions."

What can you do?

Try moving to either the left- or right-hand side of the desk to make your presentation. To reduce tension all you need to say is, "I have something to show you. Do you mind if I move around to your side of the desk?"

If the answer is "Sure, go ahead," then you have someone who is prepared to be cooperative. If the answer is "It's okay, I can see it fine from here," better dig out your bullet-proof vest. You have a sure-fire competitive situation here.

- You have only two chairs in the room and they are very close together. Message: the unspoken message about power here is something like: "I'm moving in on you."

What can you do?

Move your chair away to where you feel comfortable before you start your presentation. Try moving the chairs so they're on a diagonal to each other. Where you sit will be influenced by whether you are left- or right-handed.

LISTENING SKILLS

Active listening skills play a vital part in achieving success through reaching agreement. Studies show, however, that most people tend to be passive listeners. This means what they're doing is not so much listening as simply not talking.

The good news is that active listening, like the process of negotiating, is a skill that can be learned and practiced at every opportunity.

In most negotiations, the reason most people fail to listen is because they are too busy planning their response to what the other side is saying.

Unfortunately, the inevitable result is a poor environment for communication. If you are mentally A.W.O.L. while you're frantically deciding on your comeback to the last comment, then naturally you aren't really evaluating the essence of their message.

The result?

The very thing you're trying to avoid. Your response ends up being emotive, rather than an effective response to the issue being raised. If you're not certain just how effective your listening skills are, test them on your next internal meeting. See how much you really listen. It can be a sobering experience.

Success in the Agreement phase requires you and your team to

- communicate your message with confidence,
- listen actively, and
- respond in an appropriate manner.

There are four steps to becoming an active listener that will, if applied, increase your ability to negotiate more effectively in any situation. They are:

1. Pay attention

Force yourself to listen to what the other side is saying. This can be accomplished by

- establishing good eye contact,
- jotting down questions you need answered and ticking them off as they're answered (or highlighting them if they're not),
- leaning forward,
- taking notes,
- using positive nonverbal signals to indicate that you are paying attention—a nod, a smile—and an appropriate verbal response.

Paying attention gives you time to think about the other side's statements and lessens the risk of your responding too quickly.

2. Screen Out All Visual Distractions

Make sure that your negotiation is in an environment where visual distractions are kept to an absolute minimum.

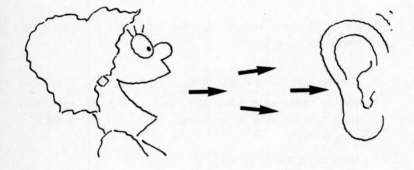

I recently went to a café to negotiate an agreement with a company over a training contract. Boy, was that a mistake! The managing director was a high-profile person; the café was very busy. Every five minutes we had to stop and say hello to one of his friends—not conducive to a good meeting. Note:

Any distraction will cause you to listen passively rather than actively.

Listening requires you to concentrate on the negotiation and not on the surroundings.

Plan a number of breaks that will allow you to rest and stay alert. It will also mean visual distractions then won't become an issue.

Screening out distractions allows you to evaluate whether there is a difference between their point of view and yours.

In short, screening out distractions helps you to concentrate and evaluate.

3. Ask Open-Ended Questions

Questions are most powerful when used in seeking clarification during the negotiation. Your questions should be phrased as concisely as possible. Waffling not only annoys the other side, it prevents you from obtaining useful information.

Ask short, focused questions that have impact.

Remember: at this point, you are looking for feelings, opinions, or reactions, not yes or no responses.

4. Listen to the Response

Ensure that you listen to the response from the other side and seek clarification if needed. Don't allow the other side to give half an answer. If you need more information for your next question, keep probing.

Don't interrupt or start talking until the other side has finished their reply. This may sound trite, but I have seen many negotiations become emotional battlefields because one side continually interrupts. Apart from its being good manners not to interrupt, it gives you the advantage of being able to respond to their whole answer, not just part of a statement. Use discipline to allow the other side airtime to respond to your questions, regardless of how painful it may become. Listening skills are the hallmark of an effective communicator. Most negotiations fail not because of the issues, but because of the ineffective communication skills being used.

Rex Ward, a sought-after management consultant in Australia, says:

"Active listening shows concern for what the other side is saying. In effect it will encourage them to say more, and speak more freely in your meeting."

Okay. The time has come when the negotiation needs to be wrapped up. Get ready to agree on the details.

You'll find this will involve you in making a number of decisions, and some of them may involve a degree of risk-taking. For instance, it might mean taking a chance with a supplier that you have never dealt with before, and saying yes to their proposal.

So be it.

You can't avoid risk totally; there's a certain amount present in any negotiation. Our hero Christopher Columbus took a big risk some 500 years ago when he set sail on his voyage of discovery. If he had turned back after twenty, twenty-five, or even thirty days because the risk was too great, certainly no one would have blamed him—but no one would have remembered him either.

You can, however, dramatically reduce the effect of risk-taking by using your negotiation Planning Sheet throughout the entire process. By having so many options to choose from, your creativity in reaching an agreement will reduce the pressure on you to take unnecessary risks.

You can, of course, decide to go outside the parameters in the Planning Sheet. But before you do, ask yourself if the risk is worth taking; after reflection, you might decide that the stake is too high. But if you do succumb and say,

"Yes, let's take the risk!"

well, stop for a moment to issue a challenge to yourself before you blithely set sail into those uncharted waters.

Why do you feel the original decisions in the Planning Sheet are no longer valid?

Are you sure it's not just a case of your feeling the heat of the moment, trying to reach an agreement with the other side pressing you hard for a decision?

If you are at all worried that this is what's happening, call a break and go back over your Planning Sheet. The other side may be applying a bit of tactical pressure so you'll say yes.

There are occasions when it's okay to go outside your Planning Sheet: there may be new information or data that makes your current Planning Sheet out of date. If that does happen, take a break so you can develop a new plan for the negotiation. It might be hard to force yourself to do that when you can smell success, but be strong! Don't rush in. Redo your Planning Sheet.

Goethe once said: "Boldness has genius, power, and magic in it!" In other words, it's good to take calculated risks, but forget those emotional risks prompted by the heat of the negotiation.

Calculating risks becomes much easier if you're aware of the proactive/reactive factor (P/R factor) in the Agreement phase of the negotiation. You'll see this P/R factor being exhibited by the participants all through a negotiation, but especially during the Agreement phase. Let's make it clearer:

THE P/R FACTOR

From a behavioral point of view, as negotiators we display many ways of behaving during a negotiation. The two main behavior styles are proactive and reactive.

During the negotiation, and specifically in the Agreement phase, both you and the other side will move along the above continuum. (You should be getting used to tacking back and forth along these imaginary lines by now. Christopher C. would be proud of you.)

PROACTIVE BEHAVIOR

This is typified by the following types of behavior in a negotiator:

Makes statements by proposing ideas, suggestions, and options during the conversation.

Sometimes asserts position aggressively through the use of logical arguments to support various points of view.

REACTIVE BEHAVIOR

You would expect to see the following behavior:

Asks questions—in fact, asks a lot of questions.

Handles any areas of disagreement in a passive way, worrying more about the feelings of the other side than the substantive issues.

It is important that you be aware of your own basic style, as it has a great impact on your willingness to take risks during a negotiation. Face it—risk-taking is a part of the negotiation that is required if you are to reach an agreement. Just make sure you're not agreeing to something you're not happy about, simply to bring things to a close.

RISK-TAKING STYLE

If, from experience, you know your P/R style is closer to the proactive end of the continuum, you tend to be a high-risk taker.

This style of negotiator is normally a person who makes forceful statements and is assertive in most of their actions. They tend to be daring and decisive in their approach to reaching agreements.

If your negotiating history shows you to be at the reactive end of the scale, you are a low-risk taker. This style of negotiator asks a lot of questions and covers every detail. They have a real need to be accurate in all decisions—even small ones, such as where to have lunch.

Regardless of your personal P/R style, you will have to move along the scale in any negotiation. Knowing where you are on the P/R continuum at any given time in the Agreement phase will influence your preparedness to take risks.

Knowing your strengths in the risk-taking area allows you to compensate for any personal limitations. For example, if you know that you are a high-risk taker, force yourself to go over the Planning Sheet before you say yes too quickly.

If, on the other hand, you know that you are a low-risk taker and struggle with every negotiation, tackle the problem head-on.

The Planning Sheet is your best friend.

Follow it closely, and as long as the other side proposes an agreement that fits your various options, be prepared to say yes and live with your decision.

Once you do reach an agreement in a negotiation, it's natural to feel that you could have hung on for a better agreement. Don't dwell on the issue of what you could have got. Make the one you have got work. The issues that you have decided upon in the Bargaining phase become valuable when you do have to take risks in the final agreement. Each issue will have a value ranking for you and the other side. You will have to be alert to decide the relative value that the other side places on each of the four main issues.

To give an example we'll return to our ever-patient house owner, hoping to make a sale to you, our Negotiator Extraordinaire.

Let's assume you have placed a high value on paying the lowest market price for the property. Being in no hurry to move in, you may have also placed a very low value on possession date.

During the Bargaining phase (where you skillfully use probing questions) you find out that the other side has placed a very high value on the possession date, as they are moving out of state.

Aha! Here's your ace up the sleeve.

The importance of the different values placed on the different issues allows you, as a negotiator, to effectively trade concessions and develop options to reach mutually satisfying agreements.

You can see how this reinforces the need for you not to give early concessions in the negotiation on any issue. There are lots of seasoned negotiators out there who believe that an early concession (of no value to you) simply stimulates the other side to behave in a similar way.

The problem is, you don't really know what is of true value in the negotiation until you find out what the four main issues are. This may not be evident until the Agreement phase. You can bet the other side will be guarding their interests carefully. The best outcome for you would be to have a concession that is highly valued by the other side, but is of low value to you. That way you have a good chance of reaching agreement without your having to take any major risks.

What if you go outside the issues on your Planning Sheet and take a risk on a point of questionable value?

For starters, you're creating a lot of stress for yourself.

Don't do it.

You won't be happy with the outcome. Stick to the plan. I can guarantee, from years of experience, that if you operate within the options you have established in your Planning Sheet:

(a) Any risks that you do take have been carefully considered.

(b) Any decision is one where you and the other side are happy to continue doing business, which builds strong relationships and trust.

It can all be a bit scary in the beginning, but once you have developed the courage to take risks in your negotiations, you will find that you will learn and grow through each experience. You might be interested to know that a recent Carnegie Foundation study report showed that one of the major indicators of sound mental health is a person's ability and willingness to take risks. Seems to me the message is clear: take risks and you won't go nuts!

Calculated risk-taking allows you to reach agreements that both you and the other side can live with. More important, it lays the foundation for working toward future agreements.

REACHING AGREEMENTS

As the negotiation draws to a close, you could find yourself going round in circles instead of reaching an agreement—if you haven't dealt decisively with any objections or concerns that the other side may have.

For example:

Let's suppose we have an accountant from a medium-sized accounting firm who is negotiating with a new customer. He has proposed a package of services. The manufacturing firm wants to say yes, but is showing some resistance in reaching agreement.

The main concern is to determine what issues are stopping the agreement from being reached.

At this stage it's imperative to get all the concerns laid out where you can see them before dealing with each objection separately.

Then handle each issue efficiently, so that both parties are happy to say yes when all the objections have been dealt with. Your listening skills will be of great importance here. Draw out the other side so that you fully understand why they are objecting—from their point of view, not yours.

Then, if you find yourself sitting there thinking "But that doesn't make sense!," consider that they might be using the "but" as a tactic to get a better deal.

If you establish that it is a genuine objection and not a tactic, you need to decide whether it's a major or minor objection.

A *major objection* is one that could be a stumbling block to your reaching an agreement. You may, say, have priced the proposal at $50,000 for the provision of the accounting services, while your nearest competitor has quoted $38,000 for the same package.

Settling major objections like this requires considerable effort before reaching the agreement. Beware of an issue being dealt with emotionally so nothing is resolved. All you end up with is a lost opportunity to create a new customer.

The real skill here is finding out what the competitor has quoted in their proposal.

Often you'll find things are not as bad as they seem—you'll be able to justify your package once you know what is being offered.

Sometimes you'll realize that what the competitor is offering is pretty much what you are offering—except that he is prepared to buy the business.

If this happens, look at your Planning Sheet; know your worst possible outcome concerning fees and be prepared to walk away.

Remember, a "no" today is better than a "no" tomorrow. Don't waste your time or company resources in areas where you are unlikely to get the business.

Think very carefully before starting to discount your fees too heavily. With great respect, if one of your strategies is to buy business at any costs, then the best of luck with staying in business.

A *minor objection* is one that can be handled quickly and without much fuss. It may be an issue raised over the commencement of services or the delivery date of the goods. It's one that can be handled without much effort.

Regardless of the concern, major or minor, ensure that you know what all the concerns are and have them all on the table before dealing with each point. Make sure you secure agreement from the other side as you deal with each issue, so you'll have no nasty surprises when you are about to shake hands on the deal.

Everyone likes to separate negotiating from selling, especially if the negotiator is part of a professional practice. Regardless of what you call this phase of the negotiation, the truth at this point is that you want the other side to say yes to your proposal.

True?

Of course it's true. So why is it that, not only in selling but in negotiating, this is the phase where up to 90 percent of salespeople or negotiators do not ask for the business or close the deal?

The reason is simple. Fear.

Fear that the other side will say no and you will suffer a personal rejection. It's essential that you remember they are saying no only to your proposal, not to you.

At this point of the negotiation you have earned the right to ask for the business. Moreover, if they say no, you have also earned the right to find out why! But try it. Ask again (and again and again!), and you will be surprised with the results.

Let's go back to the accountant we talked about earlier, who was proposing his firm's accounting services to a prospective client.

In what ways do you suppose he could ask for the business and reach an agreement? To be successful, he would need to use words and phrases that suit his own personality and style, just as you would. Put yourself in his place and try out some of the examples below to see which would best suit your unique style:

"Just suppose we could arrange our calendar to start your audit in two weeks, are you ready to give the go-ahead on our agreement?"

"If the 30-day billing terms aren't a problem for you, are you ready to approve the agreement today?"

"Okay, we've agreed on the issue over our fees. Let's wrap up the minor details; I have the authority to settle the deal now!"

Ask for the business—and you will at least be in the top 10 percent of all negotiators who have asked their way to success.

Finally, once you have asked for the business, force yourself to remain silent. This gives the other side a chance to consider your request. It also gives them a chance to say yes.

It's all too easy to talk yourself out of a deal.

Too many negotiators are so fearful of silence that they prefer to fill the room with the noise of their own talking. Whether you are doing a negotiation with one person or in a team negotiation, practice the skill of remaining silent after you have asked for the business. You won't be disappointed with the results.

The Agreement phase, when completed, is not the end of the negotiation, but the start of many new negotiations with your new business partner.

Use this phase to send out a clear message to the other side: "I'm in this deal for the long run."

Your aim is for them to walk away from the table feeling satisfied both with the deal and with the process used in reaching the deal.

SUMMARY

1. This phase is where you make detailed decisions and detailed agreements.

2. The most critical considerations in the Agreement phase are
   who is going to make the final decision,
   where the actual agreement is going to take place, and
   the timing of the agreement.

3. Be an active listener: listening skills are the hallmark of an effective communicator. Most negotiations fail not because of the issue, but because of the ineffective communication skills being used.

4. Be aware of proactive and reactive behavioral styles and their influence on risk-taking behavior: calculated risk-taking allows you to reach agreements that both you and the other side can live with. More important, it lays the foundations for working toward future agreements.

Chapter 8

Team Negotiations

*Understanding the differences in each other is the
key to successful teams.*

—Doug Malouf

If you've been involved in team negotiations yourself, you no
doubt know they can be fraught with difficulties. One person
wants to proceed carefully, consulting and checking at every step.
Another insists that it's vital to move quickly in response to a bit
of fancy footwork from the opposition. Or you could have two
different departments in the organization back home eyeing each
other suspiciously—whose concessions will be first to go?

It's true that team negotiations can present problems. Sadly,
not too many people acknowledge the tremendous benefits to
be gained.

And I assure you, there are many benefits.

Ask any champion football player.

Ask any bridge player.

You'd get the same response if you could travel back in time
and ask the Twelve Disciples recruited by Jesus of Nazareth.

Ask anyone in the dedicated teams that hunt serial killers—I'll
guarantee you'll get the same answer.

Well-organized teams who put in a genuinely cooperative effort always find that the whole is greater than the sum of its parts.

The more I mulled over the advantages of team negotiations the more I became convinced that this chapter was not an optional extra for the book. It was essential.

With the business market becoming more globally oriented every day, negotiators will need to be thoroughly skilled in acting both within and through teams.

When you start to look closely at successful team negotiations, then compare them to the disasters (as I have had cause to do on many occasions), the "pattern" for success emerges very quickly.

It's really so simple.

Successful teams are all well prepared.

Not only well prepared in terms of solid research, "what-if" scenarios, and all the other essentials we've spoken of as a recipe for success, but well prepared as a team. No evidence here of individuals all beating their own drums. Instead, they are well orchestrated—in the true meaning of the term.

To make sure each member on your team plays a counterpoint to the others, rather than overwhelming them by playing their own song, you need to be sure you understand the difference in individuals. By understanding these differences you can use them to your advantage in developing high-performance teams.

There are several aspects of team-building you need to examine:

The importance of teams in the negotiation process

The dynamics of a normal team preparation process

Problems arising in team negotiations and how to deal with them

The behavior of teams in the negotiation process

Why am I so certain that teams are more powerful than individual negotiators? Simply because I know most people honestly want to contribute at work. They want their input as a member of a team to be valued; and it is the same with a negotiation.

Before you start putting up your hand and saying "But what about. . . ?" let me say that there are occasions when the most effective way to negotiate will be on your own: a one-to-one negotiation. I'm talking, however, in generalities.

Team negotiations will increasingly become the most effective way to find mutually acceptable solutions.

In the early 1990s when Israel and the Arab world met to work out a peace accord, team negotiations undoubtedly worked. After the saber-rattling and a change of government the teams on both sides started to see progress!

It's not hard to find examples every day in the paper or on the evening news. Every time there is a major union/management negotiation, you'll see two teams hard at work presenting their respective cases, with an abundance of "experts" on both sides.

Some years ago I used to teach leadership skills in outdoor survival activities. Time after time, the group came to realize the benefits of using a cooperative team approach over the sometimes limited resources of individuals. There were always the "gung-ho" participants (yes, close relatives of the "gung-ho" negotiator) who would strive to solve the problems on their own. It was, of course, a set-up. The problems look surprisingly simple at first. The hotshots didn't bother with discussions or teamwork—they didn't need any help, no way, not them!

They never succeeded.

The activities were sneakily planned so it was impossible to solve the problems by anything other than teamwork.

Those who believed,

they had sufficient strength and knowledge to succeed on their own, or

that teams simply slowed things down,

were sentenced to failure.

It is clear that a champion team will accomplish more than a team full of different champions trying to win as separate individuals.

They learned a valuable lesson by watching a team tackle the problem and solve it. You see, being told that something is so is not the same as knowing it is so. When active learning takes place, when people learn by doing—they know.

The more you use team negotiations, the more you will realize that:

- Teams save both time and human resources when the right people are chosen.

- The great team negotiators have learned through experience that teamwork brings proceedings to a faster, more satisfying conclusion.

I learned a lot in those days of survival training. I saw first-hand, in a totally different arena from that of the business negotiation, that exactly the same principles apply in any problem-solving area. Teamwork and teams get results.

I learned something even more valuable than that, too.

I learned that to be successful, you must deal with the individuals in the team before you deal with the negotiation.

UNDERSTANDING PEOPLE

Trying to understand why people act as they do and why people respond to challenge in different ways has kept mankind fascinated for centuries.

Great writers and thinkers—Hippocrates, Carl Jung, William Marston, and others like them—have given us valuable insights into what makes others behave in certain ways. Hippocrates was one of the first to try and explain why it was important to understand individual differences. His ideas, based on medical descriptors, showed us how to assess people's behavior styles.

What does all this mean to team negotiations?

Just this:

To build a good team, you need to select people who complement each other.

Value their different communication styles; learn to use their strengths—and you can make a vital contribution to the team's success.

To you, as a team leader, the benefits of understanding and identifying the different styles of your team members are immense. When you know how people are likely to act—and react—you are in a strong position to select team members for maximum contribution to the negotiations.

Keep in mind these guidelines:

Select people for strengths that will come into their own at predetermined phases of the negotiation.

Team negotiations have a greatly increased chance of success when the team is made up of a mix of personal styles. (The usual reason for a team being made up largely of one personal style is that the team leader has tried to clone the other members of the team after him or herself.)

BEHAVIORAL STYLES

As we work our way through this chapter, I'll be using four convenient terms to describe behavioral styles based upon the work of William Marston:

1. Dominant
2. Influencing
3. Steady
4. Compliant

Like all terms, they have their drawbacks, in that you may be encouraged to brand someone as "dominant" or "compliant" on too little evidence—but if you look closely you will discover that each member of your team will actually have elements of all four behavioral dimensions in their style—but such behavior will be in different proportions.

The characteristics of each style are:

Dominance: thrives on problems and challenges; wants quick results; blunt or direct in speech.

Influencing: has the ability to influence others; warmly persuasive.

Steadiness: a good listener; steady and consistent; asks a lot of questions

Compliance: likes to follow rules and procedures; analytical and accurate; asks penetrating questions

So how will your knowledge of these styles influence your decisions as a team leader? Well, since each individual will commonly display one main behavioral style, you need to decide

how that style will impact the rest of the team, and

how it will affect the other side in the negotiating room.

Another benefit of knowing each team member's style is that it will give you a chance to see what your dominant style is in comparison with your team.

Step back a little, and try to look at the way you and your team could best work together, complementing each other's skills. Know yourself; know your team; value and use the strengths of each—and the success rate of your negotiations will astound you.

Dominant style

You will be able to identify Mr. or Ms. Dominance by their desire to get down to business immediately. They are very task-oriented in their approach. They want to know what the bottom line of the task is going to be—and they want to know right now!

Dominant negotiators tend to talk about the results they want from the project. They're raring to go, and usually want to start the negotiation immediately, even before team dynamics have been pursued. Their attitude could be expressed as follows: "Well, you're the team leader and you've chosen the team. That's as much as I want to know about the others—let's get on with business!"

Their value to your team:

Interested in bottom-line results

Quick starters, ready to go

Time is important

Prepared to solve problems

Influencing style

This type of negotiator will want to get to know the team. Mind you, it will usually be on their terms. They are quick to share who they are and where they're coming from. They're very outgoing in their behavior.

Your "influential" negotiator has a great style for the role of "ice breaker" in the first phase of team dynamics.

Mr. or Ms. Influence is usually a popular person in the organization, and you'll find they're likely to have some very good contacts if formal channels of communication break down. They're often not too strong on detail, but that's more than compensated for by their persuasive strengths.

Their value to your team:

Positive sense of humor

Good motivators when times are tough

Handle conflict creatively

Polished in presentation skills

Steadiness style

Here we have the workhorse of the team! "Steadies" are dependable types who are prepared to spend hours making sure all the information has been gathered and that it is in a usable format. They are the ultimate team players. Their listening skills are finely tuned, as they like being involved with the other team members. They would, for instance, be more useful to you in an observer's role than, say, someone of the influencing style. The "steadies" will be quite happy to listen and not comment, whereas the "influential" team player would find it almost impossible not to speak.

Their value to your team:

Empathetic listeners

Loyal team players

Excellent fact finders

Committed to leader and rest of team

Compliance style

The "compliant" type is not greatly impressed by being part of a team. Here you have someone who is quite likely to believe that the rest of the team is not up to their high standards. You'll be able to identify Mr. or Ms. Compliance by their strong analytical behavior, the precision of their actions and behavior, and the systematic preparation and delivery of their information.

If accuracy is the key to your preparation before the negotiation, then this style of negotiator will leave no stone unturned. There are pitfalls, however. You need to set clear parameters for this person— otherwise you will end up with too much information.

This type of person will not contribute much until they are satisfied it is safe to share and mix with the group. The rest of the group sometimes tend to get impatient with their high standards, but this is actually a strength if you use it correctly in relation to the team effort.

Their value to your team:

Set high standards

Conscientious and steady

Deal in areas of measurable outcomes

Thorough analysis of all tasks

It should be clearer to you now that the key to selecting your team lies first in knowing yourself and then in knowing the structure of the rest of your team.

Be careful if you have a technical negotiation.

It is tempting to have only analytical or technical people on the team, but that would be a grave error. As you can see from the different phases of a negotiation, these people might be great during the Investigative and Agreement phases—but what about the other two areas?

Look at the upcoming negotiation, decide who you need, and use their strengths to build a powerful team.

FIVE MUSTS FOR BUILDING A POWERFUL TEAM

1. Know the individuals:

It is imperative to the success of the negotiation that you select the players for your team where possible. Once you have done this, spend the time and energy to get to know them. Identify and understand their motivation toward success. Remember, money is not necessarily the main drive; it's only one of many motivators.

2. Define your expectations:

Even before you get the team together, talk to each individual and define what you expect of them in the negotiation. Let them comment on those expectations. Most teams fail because the expectations of the individuals are never clearly established at the start of the team formation. Be prepared to discuss the goals of both the organization and yourself for the negotiation.

3. Develop a big picture scenario:

The next step is to be prepared to develop the big picture with each individual. Let them know that their involvement in the process is an important part of the total negotiation. This is also an important time to let the team members know exactly what their involvement will cost them—scheduled team meetings, time away from their normal activities (or other departments), and so on.

4. Methods of assessing results:

"What's in it for me?" is the question in everybody's mind, even if they don't verbalize it. So do yourself and your team a favor—

answer the unspoken question. Indicate as early as possible the means by which the team members' results will be assessed within the organization. There should be some payoff for their time, energy, and dedication. The payoff could be money, recognition, promotion—but whatever it is, the team member should see that the negotiation is not just a disruption to their job. It's a chance to make a real contribution to the company.

5. Team members:
In team negotiations the burning issue is always the make-up of the team. Be aware that internal politics will arise very early in the discussion. Sometimes it is best to be vague about the issue until your first team meeting. Don't be tempted to play favorites, don't succumb to blackmail. Choose the best person for each part of the negotiation.

TEAM DYNAMICS

"Team dynamics" expresses the process perfectly. These two words imply that the process within a team is fast-moving and ever-changing. That is, in fact, exactly the way teams work. In every situation, a team meeting for the first time will go through four identifiable stages before they really become a team instead of a group of individuals:

1.   Ice breaker
2.   Competitive
3.   Acceptance
4.   Results

The ice breaker stage
If you want to form a team that will be effective in the long term; if you want your team members to know each other well enough to work effectively; if you want success, and the pats on the back that go with it, then you must understand that this initial stage is the most critical of all. Don't be tempted to skip it because you

have some old players on the team to "help the new ones along." Shortcuts like this will rebound on the team's effectiveness when you're all in "the hot seat."

Picture the team members meeting for the first time. One by one they walk into the room. Their different behavior styles are already dictating their responses to the situation. If you've chosen your team carefully on the basis of different talents and different styles, you'll see Ms. Influence chatting and building relationships the second she spots another team member. Mr. Steady will be looking for the leader, saying things like: "What do you want from me? Do you really think I can contribute much in a negotiation? It's not really my scene . . ."

Underneath whatever surface style they display they all feel much the same. They know their importance as individuals, but they're not so sure about being a member of a team.

This first ice-breaking stage should be a relaxed, enjoyable time not only for the team members but also for you as the group leader. Don't be tempted to go rushing into goal-setting and planning and all the rest of it just yet. The negotiation should get minimal airtime here; relationship-building is the important task. Before you finish, set a time and place for the second meeting, preferably in a less formal setting away from company premises.

Your mission as a leader in this first stage is to provide a pleasant atmosphere for the team to get to know each other before you start working on the problem. At the same time, you will be beginning to identify a mission or goal for the negotiation, and assessing the possible contributions by each of the members.

The competitive stage

It's inevitable that team members will perceive some of the team as being the "stars." Egos are on the line. Expect conflict, confusion, and a degree of resistance toward the task at hand before the dust settles.

As a team leader you should start to worry if these things are not present, because then the team is just not working as a team. Soothe ruffled feathers. Reaffirm the importance of every member of the team in their assigned role.

The acceptance stage

Here you'll breathe a little easier as you see the team move up a notch. They'll become noticeably more cohesive, and a sense of purpose and forward motion will appear. You will see the team develop parameters for making decisions. You'll see them resolving conflicts within the team and completing subtasks in an effective and speedy manner.

Watch for the situation where no member of the team wants to be seen as either negative or not involved. It's too easy to miss pinpointing the potential danger spots in the negotiation ahead if no one wants to be the one to say "I can see problems with doing it that way."

Appoint a Consequence Thinker (discussed in chapter 4) so this problem doesn't develop.

The results stage

This is the stage you've daydreamed about! Your "individuals" are now working as a team under your direction and are beginning to achieve results. To be a truly effective team leader you will encourage the team (both before and during the negotiation) to use their initiative to solve problems, and to take calculated risks in reaching decisions.

If there is a key to forging ahead successfully in this stage, it is to focus on results. Should you find you are dealing with team problems instead, you've got trouble. You're stuck in one of the other stages.

SIGNS OF TEAM TROUBLE

Even if you are a gifted leader, trouble may still arise. However, the effects of doubt, frustration, or resentment can be minimized if you keep a weather eye open for the telltale "storm brewing" signs.

Phil Shorten, a consultant and trainer in the field of developing high-performance teams, shares these useful ideas as pointers to team trouble:

1. Sometimes, your hardworking team loses sight of just how well it is performing in negotiation. This is especially true when there is a distinct lack of cooperation from the rest of the organization.

   As the team leader, it is imperative that you share the group's successes with the rest of the organization and give constant positive feedback to the team members.

2. Two related problems: frustration within the group about negotiation of their roles; and a feeling within the group that the team leader is making all the important decisions in isolation. (The issue of individual roles within a team will be discussed in detail later in this chapter.)

3. Signs of decreasing confidence: for instance, "corridor meetings" by team members after the negotiation. They may express doubts about the way the task is being handled by the leader or other team members, or you may see one or more members of the team starting to distance themselves from decisions made at the negotiating table.

4. There are delays from team members carrying out action points agreed to during the meeting.

   Any of the above signs show that team members are looking at political, personal, or professional survival.

If you see a few sparks of discontent, act quickly to put them out before they fan into brushfires that will destroy the negotiation. Meet with those individuals, ask them for their questions or concerns about the issues causing conflict. Then decide on appropriate action that will work for the whole team. You can't afford tensions like these rising to the surface at the negotiation table. Expect that things will occasionally go wrong with your team and continually monitor their performance so that you can change the tone and direction if needed.

TEAM NEGOTIATIONS

Now, let's see how your carefully structured team will fit into team negotiations.

If you are negotiating one-on-one, the style and content is more or less up to you. But team negotiations have other issues that need to be dealt with besides the issue of asking for the business.

Here are a few ideas for making team negotiations more effective and for ending up with the business instead of fighting with your own team when the other side says no.

You've seen from the examples in this book concerning negotiations that many of them are complex. They may require an investment of many months, or even years, before an agreement is reached. For this and other reasons, you'll sometimes need to involve a number of people from your company. The result is a team negotiation. It's an unfortunate fact of life that most team negotiations are handled by people who have just met. They have never had the opportunity of working together before the negotiation. I've talked to several who freely admit that, at times, they've put their case together in the car on the way to meet the other side. Such teams often use the most inexperienced person to act as note taker for the negotiation.

As you can imagine, the result is frequently disastrous.

There are both advantages and disadvantages to a team being involved in a negotiation. How can you best manage your team?

MANAGING YOUR NEGOTIATING TEAM

Team roles
Once you have

    established your team,
    set the goals, and
    developed your Planning Sheet,

you must decide which roles individuals will adopt in the negotiation.

The *Team Leader* is the role adopted by you during the negotiation. This does not necessarily mean that you will conduct the actual negotiation. Your role is to get the team working as one; planning and knowing how to execute your plans at the negotiating table.

The *Spokesperson* adopts the role of the individual who does most of the talking during the negotiation. They normally call upon the rest of the team at various stages to be involved in the discussion.

The *Numbers Person* is allotted the task of keeping track of all the facts and figures during the negotiation. As Team Leader don't ever agree to a deal until you have conferred with the Numbers Person. Sometimes what appears to be attractive at the table, when projected over five years, allows for only very small profits.

The *Specialists* are brought into the team on complex issues when legal, finance, marketing, manufacturing, or other issues may need their expert opinion or decision.

The *Observer* has possibly the most difficult role. They normally do not speak or become involved in the actual negotiation.

Their job is to observe the other side and give feedback to the team during any of the breaks throughout the negotiation. Their role is of great importance. If by chance you or the other side starts to become emotional, they can remain objective.

THE CHINESE CONNECTION

People involved in successful team negotiations will comment quite openly on their effectiveness. The team at Pickles Auctions in Australia, one of the biggest auction houses in the Southern Hemisphere, is no exception.

This is their story:

During the late 1980s Peter Pickles was faced with one of the most intriguing auctions of his career—a floating Chinese restaurant. The floating restaurant, Taipan, looked very similar to those moored all over Hong Kong, but in Sydney it was noticeably out of place. Because of a whole stack of reasons, the floating restaurant simply didn't work. The business went down the tubes, and Pickles Auctions was called in.

John Leftwich, one of the directors, got the job. He was faced with quite a task: how to auction a floating restaurant to a business environment that couldn't see the value of the vessel?

John and his team got together and decided that the most likely people to value floating cuisine would be those in the business community in Hong Kong and Singapore. They were right. Thanks to the team's efforts the vessel is now securely moored in Singapore, where patrons contentedly enjoy the local cuisine.

Good news travels fast. Shortly after, the Pickles team were approached again about a problem faced by the Chinese government. They had built the biggest and best floating Chinese restaurant for the province of Guandong, mainland China. They were confident at the time: tourism was increasing; the area was becoming prosperous and the province needed tourist attractions.

Then they found there were two problems that hadn't earned a place in their list of "what if's." The first was the massacre in Beijing—tourism dropped. The second was the fact that someone

in Guandong had built a bridge over the river and the floating restaurant couldn't get to its designated mooring place.

They were faced with a dual dilemma: the bank that had financed the deal wanted its money: the People's Republic of China didn't want the floating restaurant.

Who could they call? That's right: the team from Pickles Auctions, in Australia.

Over many months of hard negotiating, the Pickles team won the right to auction the floating restaurant. It meant a greater commitment from the Pickles team, since nearly all negotiations were carried out in Guandong Province. John was not only away from Australia but, for the most part, away from his original team.

He has no doubt whatsoever about the value of his team.

"The deal would not have been struck without the international team I assembled," says John firmly. "The biggest thing was being able to build trust with the other side and show that my team could handle the job."

John's speed in responding, the preparation before the deal, and his ability to negotiate on his feet at all times resulted in the deal being struck and the floating restaurant being sold.

Furthermore, this was a great historical moment as this was the first Chinese government asset ever sold by the auction system.

When they work in harmony, teams are powerful.

SUMMARY

1. To establish the foundations of a powerful, dynamic team, follow these simple suggestions:

   Pick the best possible team.

   Don't clone them in your likeness.

   Try to have the strengths of each style represented in your group.

2. Negotiating teams are powerful tools. Become practiced in the use of teams in any major negotiation: the global market demands more team negotiations, and you will have a competitive edge over your competition.

Chapter 9

The Creative Negotiator!

*The human mind once stretched by a new idea,
never regains its original dimensions.*

—Oliver Wendell Holmes

When you pick up books with titles like *A Whack on the Side of the Head* and *How to Unlock Your Mind for Innovation*, your interest is piqued before you even open them. Without having read a word, you are expecting something different. Roger Von Oech has just given you the first clue about the value he places on creativity.

If you attend one of Roger's seminars, the next sixty-four clues come tumbling one after the other as he walks around handing out cards from his *Creative Whack Pack*.

Creative Whack Pack? A Whack on the Side of the Head?

What is this, a karate convention gone mad?

No. It's just one man's creative way of challenging our conventional modes of thinking. One man who knows the value of creativity and innovation in the business world and has thought of a unique way of focusing our attention on it.

The sixty-four cards in Roger Von Oech's *Creative Whack Pack* are designed solely to get your creative juices flowing; to get you to step out of your habitual way of thinking.

The message he delivers—that there are many ways of looking at a situation—has the same significance for those of us involved in negotiating as it has for business in general.

Roger Von Oech's thoughts about creativity are all the more inspiring because of his originality in packaging the message.

Consider, for example, the *Whack Pack* card that I looked at during one of his seminars: I scanned the story on it and the message hit home at once.

I suspect the story has a message for most businesspeople; so let me present his intriguing little tale, and see what you get out of it:

In days long gone, small villages in Europe sometimes fell victim to strange plagues. One particular plague left its victims in a death-like coma, and death normally followed some twenty-four hours later. It was only after a couple of lucky townsfolk magically recovered while they were awaiting burial that the villagers realized with horror that they had no doubt buried a few victims alive.

They held a hurried conference. What were they going to do?

Thankfully, the majority decided it was best to put food and water in the coffin so if the victims were still alive, at least they would survive. This was creative and the classic win/win scenario for everyone (especially for the person in the coffin).

But the plan did not meet with universal approval. The villagers were poor, and some objected. A cheaper solution was put forward. (A classic "quick fix," in fact.)

Why not, they suggested, implant a foot-long stake in every coffin lid directly over the victim's heart? Once the coffin lid was closed—no more worries! The plague victim had no chance of being buried alive.

The story was designed to make the reader think about the type of questions that might be asked in any given situation and to look carefully at solutions. Look carefully at the way you interpret any available information.

You can readily see how this applies to negotiating.

Always look for a creative approach that will lead to a win/win situation. Your ability to be creative is largely decided by your personal view of the negotiating situation. Do you see it as a battle of egos? As a situation where victory goes to the toughest or the biggest? Or as a process whereby better agreements can be reached?

If you're the type of negotiator who views the negotiation process as a starting point for a long-term relationship with your customers, you're well set for a creative approach.

In other words, it's the "food and water" approach, in preference to the "quick fix" foot-long stake through the heart.

Taking this view will allow you to adopt a flexible, creative approach in the negotiation. It will give you a chance to create many options, so that both sides can come to a successful conclusion.

As we rush toward the year 2000 and beyond, the whole issue of creativity—not only in negotiating, but in every facet of a business—will determine whether or not your organization will survive or become a statistic. We all have to try to create an environment that is conducive to creativity, both for ourselves and our particular teams.

We spoke in the last chapter about the power of using teams in the negotiating process. Let's have a look at an example of how teamwork can turn around an entire country's productivity.

Some years ago, the United States started becoming concerned about its trade imbalance. The situation worsened with Japan's surge to the front line as a market leader in consumer products, automobiles, manufacturing, and the steel industry. The problem needed more than money or increased production time thrown at it; it needed an entirely new, creative approach.

Finally, about a decade ago, American companies started to turn the tide. They began to turn out quality products, not solely through superior technology, but also by empowering the workers to make decisions and to become part of a productive team.

The resulting improved trade situation is an example of how management and workers made an effort to work together to create a future through quality products, sustained growth in their industry, and a secure place in the market.

Cooperation such as this between management and workers is steadily on the increase worldwide. The path to creative problem-solving is not (and has not been) smooth. Entrenched unions—worried that such teams will be unilaterally structured by management—haven't accepted change quietly. However, as more cases of enterprise bargaining culminate in advantages for both workers and management, the changes are becoming not only tolerated but welcomed.

One such case was the eleven-point agreement struck between workers and employees at the SPC plant in Shepparton, Victoria, Australia, in January 1991.

Despite a storm of publicity, the workers were happy to agree to what they considered a win/win scenario—SPC, after four years in the red, would save millions of dollars and the workers would save their jobs. The board had gone from desperation to victory—by presenting the stark facts to the workers and asking for their cooperation in working out a deal to save the company. After meeting for many long hours, management and SPC shop stewards ended up turning accepted work practices and conditions inside out to find savings of the two and a half million dollars needed to keep the banks on their side.

The workers accepted the fact that they would lose initially, by having to sacrifice such things as holidays, vacation time, and payment of overtime for weekend work. On the plus side, they would not face unemployment and could look forward to permanent profit-sharing as a trade-off.

In 1992, profit-sharing was to become a reality. Now the history-making SPC agreement is being promoted as an example of the new flexibility available to workers and employers.

John Corboy, SPC's chairman, put it simply:

"It was a situation of real need that had to have a solution."

Creative though such negotiations may be, it is inevitable that on some occasions Murphy's Law will ensure that even the most promising solutions fall apart right in front of our eyes.

Often we are unwilling to believe it. There are groans all round. "What happened?" we ask, stunned. "Our preparations have been second to none; we've followed all the steps; tried to be creative . . . what went wrong?" It's probably happened to all of you at least once. (If it hasn't, it will.) There'll always be Murphy's Law to stand in the way of a brilliant deal.

The things that can unexpectedly go wrong may be large problems or small, but they all make us want to punch walls.

I can't offer you a solution—there isn't one—for a "wild card" situation, but:

You'll be better able to face whatever "Murphy" throws at you if you follow the negotiation process outlined in this book, step by step. Be as comprehensively prepared as possible, ensuring that you have numerous options so that you can be flexible in your decisions. If the negotiation turns out to be a case of Murphy's Law—well, them's the breaks!

Don't ever lose sight of the fact that both sides want to win.

Approach your negotiation in a spirit of fairness and cooperation, genuinely wanting both sides to win. By doing this you can ensure that the negotiation truly embraces the Deliberate style on the continuum. Every action, every deal, is designed to enhance the long-term relationship with the customer with whom you are negotiating. Even if you "lose" this negotiation, you'll be the ultimate winner. You'll have respect, and a reputation not only for fairness, but for creativity in proposing win/win solutions. That's not a bad reputation to have!

It would be nice if the other side in all negotiations could operate like that, wouldn't it? Our stress levels would fall dramatically. Oh well, we live in the real world, not Fantasyland. And sometimes the other side simply does not want to negotiate.

What do you do then?

What do you do when it seems the matter can't be resolved?

Sometimes, you may find yourself wondering desperately: "why negotiate at all?"

WHY NEGOTIATE?

When I ran a four-day negotiating skills conference for a group of senior IBM marketing managers and representatives, the group was highly motivated. They were working in an interesting market, and they were dead keen to find creative ways to negotiate. The conference was as stimulating for me as it was for them.

During a break, one of the participants came up to me.

"What you say is interesting," he said, "but I have to ask something. Why do you bother to go on with a negotiation if the other side is stuck on price and won't move?"

"Fair question," I allowed. "Well, the conclusion I've come to over the years is that if they weren't interested in your offer, they wouldn't be still talking to you. They would have thrown you out long since."

"I guess there's sense in that." Apparently satisfied, he wandered off to get coffee.

He has not been the first to ask that sort of question. At the end of a long day of negotiations where the other side appears immovable on price, many of us would like nothing better than to throw up our hands, say "forget it!," and go home. Doing something like that might relieve stress in the short term. There's a downside to such action, though.

First, you'll have a nagging sense of failure and frustration because you gave up.

Second, you would be throwing away the opportunity to look at the issues more creatively and come up with an alternative solution that suits everyone.

Play it right down to the wire. As long as they're still talking, they're still interested. Admittedly, it takes more work and commitment to look for the creative solution. Maybe a whack on the side of the head is what we all need now and again to jolt tired brain cells into thinking of original solutions!

Can you remember the last time during one of your negotiations when the solution to a problem seemed not only complex but totally related to price issues?

Where was the difficulty?

Were the "solutions" offered mundane and predictable?

Did anyone attempt to come at the problem from a completely different perspective?

As you go over the issue in your mind now, do you think it's possible that all that was needed was a bit of lateral thinking? Can you think of any way out that did not occur to you at the time?

Get it firmly fixed in your mind now:

Most problems, including price issues, can be negotiated if both sides are looking for an answer. Having said all this, I admit that inevitably some negotiations will become deadlocked. The International General Agreement on Tariffs and Trade (GATT) talks are a perfect example of what can happen if one side in a negotiation has a hidden agenda or no real desire to reach an agreement in the first place.

The GATT talks were designed to overcome problems of agricultural subsidies and protectionism being afforded to farmers by some of the trading partners. The Uruguay round of trade talks began in Punta del Este in 1986 and finally broke down in December 1990, when the European community failed to remove major farm subsidies granted to their farmers.

The participants in the GATT talks were ostensibly looking to a mutually satisfactory plan for the future for all trading partners. For some of the negotiators, "mutually satisfactory" was interpreted as "as long as we are satisfied."

By early 1992, observers were cynically betting that the talks would not be resolved before the turn of the century! By late 1992, the United States fired the first salvo in trying to break up the impasse over the trade talks. The result of that impasse is now history.

There is a lesson to be learned from the GATT talks that you can apply to your business negotiations. If we assume that both sides genuinely want to reach an agreement, the time for conflict about price, delivery, quality, or whatever is at the Bargaining phase of the negotiation, not the end. This holds whether the negotiation involves your number-one account customer or a group of staff members with whom you have to negotiate a new salary agreement.

When you analyze the slowdown of the negotiation process in situations like the GATT talks, the biggest problem soon becomes obvious. Dig deeper than the surface bickering, and you'll be looking at the real killer—the failure of the communication process on both sides.

Clear communication is something that we wrestle with in every facet of our lives—it's not only in a negotiation that communication is a problem! Marriage counselors have waiting lists of couples with communication problems; magazines run article after article on opening up lines of communication between parents and children or workers and management. Scan the "Help Wanted" pages in your local newspaper and you'll soon see how many ads list "excellent oral and written communication skills" as "essential." Lack of skill in communicating is the biggest block to effective employer/employee relations—so why wouldn't the same problem rear its head in the world of negotiating?

Analyze the causes of failure at the negotiating table, and you'll find that it's lack of communication that destroys the negotiation as much as the issues that everyone's fighting about.

If you want to minimize the chances of this happening to you, then try to establish a win/win situation by concentrating on the people issues.

Every negotiation is ultimately about people.

Communication skills are a vitally important part of the effective negotiator's repertoire. To be a creative negotiator, you need to be a person who has a range of skills that are used successfully during the whole process. You need to have the ability to build trust and relationships throughout the negotiation.

This may sound like a tall order, but stop for a moment and think about the top negotiators you know.

Why do they close deals consistently?

Why do they have the other side coming back for more?

Learn from these men and women who have tapped the secrets of successful negotiation. They win because they are adaptable negotiators with a range of skills and knowledge about human behavior. In the global marketplace of today, you'll find competitive forces coming at you from every side. You need to be quick and responsive in analyzing these forces before, during, and after each negotiation.

It's the negotiator who applies creative ways to solve problems who will continue to reach agreement even in the toughest of negotiations.

Creative negotiators don't view issues as roadblocks, they view them as opportunities for a solution to be reached. Often, people have no idea of their true capacity for original solutions until they're asked to consider unusual ways around a problem. So, in my training sessions, I try to give people the opportunity to flex their creative muscles.

As an example, try the quick quiz on page 200.

Time after time, I've noticed the difference in results when *participants actively look for creative ways around problems.*

Every time this happened, they not only came up with better solutions than the "obvious" ones that occurred the first time around, but, also thought of ideas and innovations to solve other problems in their organization or their particular negotiation.

In these situations it's particularly noticeable that teamwork seems to encourage creativity and generates a powerful energy to solve problems. Over the years I've worked with many creative negotiators—talented people who are committed to better solutions not some of the time, but all of the time. It would be impossible to pick out the best: how do you choose among people who

HOW MANY SQUARES CAN YOU SEE?

Please record your number: _____
(See page 205 for answer.)

operate in different environments, under different constraints, with different agendas?

There are, however, two teams of negotiators whose actions under pressure were so impressive that the memory of their creativity still inspires and motivates me. One team (American) has achieved worldwide recognition. The other team—Pickles

(Australian)—may not be as well known, but the memory of what it was like to work with such a stimulating crew will remain with me for many years to come.

Robert Edward Turner III, founder and president of Cable News Network (CNN), a global TV news company, was named *Time*'s Man of the Year for 1991.

If I wanted to outline all of Robert Turner's achievements, it would take many more pages than I have available here. What is relevant in this chapter is his ability to develop a creative environment within his corporation that spills over into global negotiations by his executives.

None of us are likely to forget the graphic TV coverage of the start of the "mother of all battles," the Gulf War of 1990–91.

Confess: you, too, were glued to your seat day after day watching War As It Happened, weren't you? You, too, shared that awful this-can't-be-happening feeling. You, too, wondered how the world would come out of this war.

We owe that amazing coverage to the exceptional negotiation skills shown by executives from CNN. Just days before the battle started, they put a tremendous amount of time and energy into negotiating special transmitting facilities out of Baghdad, ready for the war that seemed inevitable.

It was a masterpiece of negotiation. With war looming ever closer, negotiations had to be fast, yet decisions could come only after careful planning and consideration. A delicate balance of speed and care: one slip and it's over. CNN spent hundreds of thousands of dollars securing the telecommunications link they needed with the outside world.

Did this care, foresight, and massive commitment of funds pay off?

Well, you saw the results. All the other stations from around the world, relying on the conventional telephone systems, found themselves cut off immediately.

CNN reigned supreme.

Like millions of people who never strayed more than a few steps from their TV screens or radios once the war began, I was consumed by the graphic details coming from the CNN reporters in Baghdad.

Everyday concerns seemed irrelevant. In the first few hours of the war, while listening to the radio, I drove into a car wash with the aerial up on my new car. One bent aerial and one hundred dollars later, I was able to keep listening.

It was a magnificent coup for CNN. They were able to utilize the technological advances of the eighties to provide people all over the world with images of war, live, virtually minute by minute—without going into moral issues.

What soap opera or action movie could compete with that?

A triumph of negotiation, indeed!

But there are, of course, the gifted negotiators operating on a more local level. If you want to find a team of hardworking, risk-taking, brilliantly creative negotiators, pay a visit to Peter Pickles and his team at Pickles Auctions.

The executives who make up this team are some of the most persistent, and perhaps the craziest, negotiators I have ever worked with.

Crazy? Doesn't that contradict everything I've said about careful preparation and judicious weighing of alternatives?

Not at all.

I say "crazy" because of the pace and energy radiating from their creative way of adapting, minute by minute, to the demands of the negotiation process; their lightning-fast assessments of risk factors and swift decisions to act. The Pickles team wholeheartedly support Tom Peters's view that time is the most critical element in corporate success. Decisions are made on the run: no memos, no committees, just real-time, down-to-earth decisions— and they work.

Like the CNN team, Peter Pickles and his executives view negotiations as fluid situations. They're prepared for change. While I watched, they took swiftly calculated risks and finally closed a creative deal where the outcome was eminently acceptable for both parties.

The Wrap-Up

What a sense of jubilation and accomplishment Columbus and his crew must have felt on the day that they sighted land. All the hard work and risks had been worth it. Isn't that how you would like to feel after every negotiation? It's how you will feel, if you have

    done your investigative work,

    prepared your Planning Sheet,

delivered a dynamic proposal, and

creatively sought an agreement.

At last, you can say yes to the final deal being offered and be happy with your decision.

Having been closely involved with negotiations both large and small for years, I wasn't surprised to have my feelings about skillful negotiations confirmed when (1) researching this book and (2) observing the great negotiators. It has been obvious to me for some time that the great negotiators have four skills that distinguish them from the crowd.

FOUR "KNOW-HOW'S" OF A GREAT NEGOTIATOR

1. Creativity
2. Versatility
3. Motivation
4. The ability to walk away

Check these skills against your own. While you're doing it, think about why each skill is so important for the successful negotiator. Take a moment to reflect upon those negotiations in which you've been involved in recent months and ponder on the good ones.

Did those negotiators demonstrate versatility and motivation? Were they prepared to exercise the "Walk-Away" option? Why did you feel satisfied at the end of the deal? Why would you have felt happy to negotiate with them again? Think about your answers to these questions. Then think carefully about using these creative negotiators as role models.

Creativity
What was your answer to the forty-square exercise? To be more creative, read this chapter again and again. Read widely from

other sources, too, such as the books of Edward de Bono, which are renowned for their innovative suggestions.

Cultivate an open and inquisitive mind.

Versatility

Being versatile in and during a negotiation means having the ability to think and move quickly on your feet. CNN demonstrated that ability by their lightning-swift negotiations to gain the transmitter—and in the process made themselves a household name around the world.

They had done their homework.

Pickles Auctions had done theirs.

Both teams knew that the up-front investment in preparing for the negotiation put them into a strong position from the start.

Versatility sometimes requires that you be almost visionary in your negotiations. It means you have to be ready to ride the waves of change during the process. To do that, you really need to view the Planning Sheet as a guideline.

If the information changes, then redo your Planning Sheet.

This will allow you to stay versatile. Such versatility allows you to work on the things that you can influence and forget about the ones you can't. What's the point in worrying about things over which you have no control?

I sometimes see executives in consulting projects get so caught up in anxiety that their stress levels soar and they become virtually paralyzed. Their versatility is shackled and so, unfortunately, is their effectiveness. Versatility essentially means being able to take a rational overview of any negotiation and getting the best deal under the circumstances.

(Note: Not necessarily the best price, but the best deal.)

Here's a personal example of a time when versatility was the order of the day:

My wife, Gillian, and I started looking for a home at the start of a boom in property values, and after two long months had viewed about sixty different homes. In a state of shock, we watched prices rising, on average, between four and seven thousand dollars (depending on the suburb) each week. The market seemed totally crazy.

Sometimes up to fifty people were waiting to attend an "open house" inspection. It was common to arrive at a property and see anxious buyers rush in, look around, and hastily say, "I'll buy it!" to the waiting agent. It was just as common to see desperate purchasers (terrified they would miss out on a property) start an auction, wildly offering more money.

Normally sane adults started to behave in a way that would not be tolerated in children. Anger and frustration gave rise to hot-tempered accusations or feelings of despair. During this time the leeway to negotiate on price was almost nil. The chance of being versatile in discussions seemed impossible.

Our spirits sank lower and lower.

One night we saw a small advertisement for a three-bedroom villa, one in a block of seven. When I called the agent, I found that the properties had been put on the market three days before. Now, just one property remained.

"If we make a quick decision," I said to the agent (with fingers crossed), "and can settle immediately, what room do we have to negotiate?"

He laughed. "None," he said pityingly. "The price is as advertised."

Knowing the market as we did, it was the answer we had expected. I would have replied in the same way. So, knowing that we could not influence the price negotiation, we had to be versatile, not them.

It was time to sit down and think what, if anything, we could gain. We talked to the agent and discovered that the developer needed the cash urgently. It was the only ace we held.

There wasn't a lot we could do, except settle at the speed of light to prevent anyone outbidding us.

Versatility in a negotiation is knowing when you can influence a decision and when you can't—for example:

THE VERSATILITY MODEL

CAN INFLUENCE	CAN'T INFLUENCE
Your presentation	Their team makeup
Your research	Their acceptance of facts
Your questions	Their responses

The list could go on, but essentially:

Being versatile means having the ability to know when and how you can influence the other side's decision and knowing when to have the patience to let them do their part in the process.

Motivation

We have spoken at great length throughout the book on what motivates you in a negotiation. You need to give equal thought to what motivation the other side brings to the bargaining table.

We saw a classic example of different motivational needs during the United Nations/Iraq war. Night after night, we watched the CNN coverage to see if Saddam Hussein would release the hostages he was using as a human shield.

Friends and relatives made public pleas to the government to do something.

Initial attempts to have the hostages released revolved around payment for their release. Important people from around the world visited Baghdad and Kuwait, trying to negotiate their freedom.

It proved to be the wrong approach, because Saddam's motivation to negotiate was not guided by monetary gain. What he wanted was international coverage of "Saddam the Compassionate" releasing hostages in full view of the world.

Those early visits to Baghdad were fruitless because the negotiators did not understand the dominant motivation for the other

side to say yes. Saddam didn't want money. He wanted international propaganda.

Never forget, money is only one issue of many during the negotiation. It is essential for your negotiating success that you don't get caught up in thinking it's the only one!

There are many theories promulgated on motivation, but the process that I will share with you now is simple and can be applied to any situation:

First: Identify the dominant need of the other side. Know what it is, because then and only then do you stand a chance of reaching agreement. For instance, if the other side has a cash flow problem, their immediate need is cash. Security comes later.

Second: Know what the other side considers to be a reasonable payoff. Their final decision to say yes will be geared to the value that they will place on the payoff. For example: a deal may be struck on an asset that may have a reduced value over time. By offering a larger cash deposit than normal, the deal could be secured.

Third: Understand the risk level of the other side in reaching an agreement. Forget the risk from an organizational point of view: concentrate on the personal risk to the negotiators themselves. If they can live with the risk to themselves, then they will start looking at the impact the negotiation will have on the organization.

Once you have a clear picture of the other side based on these understandings, you will start to get a fairly clear idea of their reasons for negotiating in the first place.

The next step is to achieve the same level of understanding about yourself, then about your team. If you can't identify the dominant need, the payoff, and the risk level for both sides, then the message is clear: don't negotiate.

The Walk-Away

You can bet that as soon as people know that you specialize in a particular area, they all want that one free "secret," or idea, to fix their problems.

Kermit Boston, for example, is a trainer and specialist in the area of understanding people. He is constantly asked the quickest way to interpret the actions of the other side in a negotiation. People love to find a "quick fix."

It's no different for me. The minute people find out that negotiating is one of my areas of specialty they always want to know a quick tip to make them a better negotiator.

This is what I tell them (there, you didn't even have to ask!):

Negotiating the "Quick Fix"—Say No!

> *The number-one skill that all negotiators must have*
> *is the ability to walk away from a deal and say NO!*

If you close this book with that idea firmly in your mind, the cost of this book will become just a drop in an ocean of savings for you and your business.

Yes, the Walk-Away does involve risk-taking. The ability to make an intelligent decision (sometimes in the face of overwhelming odds), to stand up and walk away from the negotiating table, has to contain some element of risk.

However, always remember that walking away is easy once you have prepared your negotiating Planning Sheet.

Having done that, you always know when you have reached your Worst Possible outcome.

I would even go so far as to say that, armed with your Planning Sheet, you can walk away without fear. Without your Planning Sheet you have to battle your ego—and guess what? The ego normally wins!

Knowing the Worst Possible outcome, and having the ability to stand up and leave, will put you and your business on the fast track toward success.

We started with Columbus, so let's finish with Columbus. A great adventurer has shown us the way in a book on negotiating skills. Christopher Columbus showed immense perseverance and discipline in dealing with the royal family in Spain.

Learn from him.

You'll find that most deliberate negotiations will go down this same track. Like Columbus, great negotiators know that it is the hackwork, the late nights, the long meetings that eventually pay off.

It's choosing a Consequence Thinker for your Preparation phase that will help you develop a winning proposal.

It's having the ability to flow with the changes in the negotiation: twenty days out from Madrid, Columbus's crew were revolting (the verb, not the adjective). Did he give up? No. He sought solutions. You, like Columbus, must be able to handle that type of situation in a negotiation.

Persevere—because each step, no matter how small, is leading to success. Know that it won't be plain sailing all the way: be prepared to trim the sails and change course, and like Columbus, you will find that your negotiating know-how will develop at a rate of knots!

Throughout this book, example after example has shown you how you can successfully negotiate anything—from the price of a refrigerator to an international agreement. By following the series of clearly outlined steps we have shown you; by watching for pitfalls; and most of all by cultivating your creativity—you, too, can be a master negotiator!

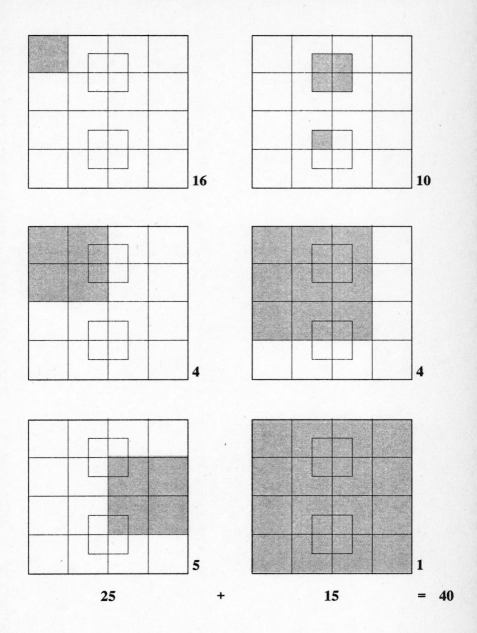

16

10

4

4

25   +   15   = 40

5   1

Bibliography

Authors, many and varied. *Living Bible*. Wheaton, IL: Tyndale House, and Youth for Christ.

Covey, Stephen. *The Seven Habits of Highly Effective People*. New York: Simon and Schuster, 1979.

De Bono, Edward. *Six Thinking Hats*. New York: Little, Brown, 1985.

Fisher, Roger, and Scott Brown. *Getting Together*. Boston: Houghton Mifflin, 1988.

Fisher, Roger, and William Ury. *Getting to Yes*. Boston: Houghton Mifflin, 1991.

Hanzhang, General Tao. *Sun Tzuí's Art of War*. New York: Sterling, 1987.

Hickman, Craig, and Michael Silva. *Creating Excellence*. New York: New American Library, 1984.

Kennedy, Gavin. *Doing Business Abroad*. New York: Simon and Schuster, 1985.

Kennedy, Gavin. *Field Guide to Negotiation*. New York: McGraw-Hill, 1985.

Kepner, Charles H., and Benjamin Tregoe. *The New Rational Manager*. Princeton, NJ: Princeton Research Press, 1981.

Knowles, Malcolm S. *Andragogy in Action*. San Francisco: Jossey-Bass, 1984.

Mackay, Harvey. *Swim with the Sharks*. New York: Morrow, 1988.

Mackenzie, Alec. *The Time Trap*. New York: AMACOM, 1990.

Marsten, William Mailter. *Emotions of Normal People*. Minneapolis: Reisona Press, 1979.

Nierenberg, Gerard I. *The Art of Negotiating*. New York: Pocket Books, 1984.

Nierenberg, Gerard I. *The Complete Negotiator*. New York: Nierenberg and Zeif, 1986.

Odiorne, George S. *The Human Side of Management*. Lexington, MA: Lexington Books, 1987.

Parker, Glenn M. *Team Players and Teamwork*. San Francisco: Jossey-Bass, 1990.

Peters, Thomas J., and Robert H. Waterman Jr. *In Search of Excellence*. New York: Harper and Row, 1982.

Peters, Tom, and Nancy Austin. *A Passion for Excellence*. New York: Random House, 1985.

Phillips, Steven R., and William H. Bergquist. *Solutions—A Guide to Better Problem Solving*. San Diego, CA: University Associates, 1987.

Porter, Michael E. *The Competitive Advantage of Nations*. New York: Free Press, 1990.

Yasuda, Yuzo. *40 Years, 40 Million Ideas*. Cambridge, MA: Productivity Press, 1991.

Index

political and economic
policies, 70-71, 82
internal
  corporate goals, 67-68
  departmental relationships,
    68, 81
  formal structure, 66-67, 81
  informal structure, 67, 81
  personal relationships, 68-69, 81
  unions, 69-70
internal and external, 59, 64-65
Eye contact. *see also* Body
language; Communication skills
and seating arrangement, 142, 145

F
Fallback positions, 63, 64.
  see also Negotiating process
Fear. *see also* Nervousness;
  Self-confidence
communication of, 27
of public speaking, 50, 59
reducing, 86
of rejection, 156-157
Flexibility, in planning, 72, 76, 82
Foreign negotiations, roles for, 59

G
General Agreement on Tariffs and
  Trade (GATT), 189-190
Global market, 22
Goals. *see also* Needs
corporate, 35, 64, 67-68, 81
establishing, 29
satisfying, 35
Government, cooperation with
  private sector, 40, 42
Gulf War, 193-194, 199

H
Habits, 37, 132
Hollywood classics. *see* Tactics
Home buying model, 73-75, 88-89,
  134, 152, 198

Hot line, 32
*How to Create and Deliver a
Dynamic Presentation* (Malouf),
92, 96
*How to Unlock Your Mind for
Innovation* (Von Oech), 183

I
Illustrations
charts and graphs, 102-104
  bar chart, 104
  block diagrams, 104
  line chart, 103
  pie chart, 103
  schematics and scale
    drawings, 104
  tables and columns, 104
in presentation, 96-101
presentation techniques,
  105-108, 143
  body language, 106-108
  overlay technique, 105
  pointer use, 105
  revelation technique, 105
  scheduling, 106
  35mm slides, 101, 105-106
Information, giving away in
  presentations, 110, 123, 126
Information gathering. *see also*
Planning; Preparation;
Questions
benefits of, 65, 67, 71
excess information, 87-88
with questions, 134
Integrity, discussed, 29
International marketplace, 66, 70-71.
  see also Cultural negotiations
Interruptions, 147-148
Intimidation, in seating
  arrangement, 142
Investigative phase, 49, 52,
  56, 61. *see also* Negotiation
model
discussed, 63-83

Presentations
by Daria Price Bowman

In today's business world, it's extremely important to effectively communicate your ideas. Whether you're selling a product, outlining a proposal, or attempting to generate support for a project, a superior presentation will get superior results.

Presentations offers step-by-stop instructions on developing and delivering the perfect presentation, including how to:

- Organize your speech and perfect your delivery
- Assess and engage your audience
- Select visual aids that capture your audience's attention
- Use your surroundings to maximize the impact of your presentation
- Field questions and use them to your advantage

With its easy-to-apply, tried-and-true methodology, *Presentations* is an indispensable guide for anyone who needs to get an important point across.

Trade paperback
ISBN: 1-55850-798-1, $9.95
5½" x 8½", 224 pages

Available Wherever Books Are Sold

If you cannot find these titles at your favorite retail outlet, you may order them directly from the publisher. BY PHONE: Call 1-800-872-5627 (in Massachusetts 781-767-8100). We accept Visa, Mastercard, and American Express. $4.50 will be added to your total order for shipping and handling. BY MAIL: Write out the full titles of the books you'd like to order and send payment, including $4.50 for shipping and handling, to: Adams Media Corporation, 260 Center Street, Holbrook, MA 02343. 30-day money-back guarantee.

Time Management
by Marshall J. Cook